THE BEST OF BERLIN IN 6 WALKS

WALK 1 > MITTE p. 18

Mitte is the beating heart of Berlin. It's situated around the border between East and West and is where you'll find the most important sights, shopping streets, and many unique restaurants.

WALK 2 > PRENZLAUER BERG p. 38

This neighborhood underwent a complete facelift after the Wall fell. Once a typical workers' district, it's now one of the most sought-after residential areas in the city. Looking for the perfect Kaffee und Kuchen? This is where to go.

WALK 3 > FRIEDRICHSHAIN p. 58

In this alternative neighborhood, old so-called 'Ossi's' live side-by-side with punks, up-and-coming artists, and students. This area alongside the river Spree is lively and fun.

WALK 4 > CHARLOTTENBURG & SCHÖNEBERG p. 78

Charlottenburg is back: The once-deteriorated area around the Bahnhof Zoo is bustling again. It was in Schöneberg where John F. Kennedy spoke his legendary words: "Ich bin ein Berliner."

WALK 5 > KREUZBERG p. 98

This district is divided into two parts. "36" is more colorful and gritty, while "61" is the quieter of the two, with small streets, green parks, and beautiful museums.

WALK 6 > NEUKÖLLN p. 118

Neukölln is up and coming and changing every day. Tempelhofer Freiheit is a favorite destination, but don't miss the less famous parts, like Schillerkiez and Rixdorf.

BERLIN WALKS

Step off the plane and head straight for the newest, hippest coffee joint in town. Find out where you can get the best *Currywurst* in the city or where they have locally brewed beer on tap. *Moon Berlin Walks* lets you in on all the hotspots and Berlin's best kept secrets. This way, you can skip the busy shopping streets and stroll through the city at your own pace, taking in a local attraction on your way to the latest and greatest shops. Savor every second and make your trip a truly great experience.

BERLIN-BOUND!

You're about to discover Berlin, the city of East and West, Checkpoint Charlie, the Brandenburger Tor and the Reichstag, *Biergartens* and *Currywurst*, creative spirits, and linen bags. We love Berlin's diverse neighborhoods. They have their own unique vibe, sights, shops, and restaurants. Do you like art and history, or would you rather hit some stores? Maybe you want to party until the wee hours of the morning? Whatever your fancy, there's a perfect neighborhood for you and good food at every turn. Follow us—we'll show you where to go.

ABOUT THIS BOOK

In this book, local authors share with you the genuine highlights of their city. Discover the city by foot and at your own pace, so you can relax and experience the local lifestyle without having to do a lot of preparation beforehand. That means more time for you—what we call "time to momo." Our walks take you past our favorite restaurants, cafés, museums, galleries, shops, and other notable attractions—places we ourselves like to go.

None of the places mentioned here have paid to appear in either the text or the photos, and all text has been written by an independent editorial staff. This is true for the places in this book as well as for the information in the **time to momo app** and all the latest tips, themed routes, neighborhood information, blogs, and the selection of best hotels on **www.timetomomo.com.**

CITY
BERLIN

WORK & OTHER ACTIVITIES
PHOTO EDITOR

LOCAL
MAARTJE VAN OURS

During her first year in Berlin, Maartje discovered every corner, park, and Hinterhof in Mitte and Prenzlauer Berg. Not only can she tell you where to eat and drink (her latest obsession is Der Laden), but she'll also be able tell you all about the old building across the street. She ensures her 94-year-old granddad, hip 25-year-old sister, and friends alike all have a good time.

PRACTICAL INFORMATION

The six walks in this book allow you to discover the best neighborhoods in the city by foot and at your own pace. The walks will take you past museums and notable attractions but, more importantly, they'll show you where to go for good food, drinks, shopping, entertainment, and an overall good time. Check out the map at the front of this book to see which areas of the city the walks will take you through.

Each route is clearly indicated on a detailed map at the beginning of the relevant chapter. The map also specifies where each place is located. The color of the number tells you what type of venue it is (see the key at the bottom of this page). A description of each place is given later in the chapter. Without taking into consideration extended stops at various locations, each walk will take a maximum of three hours. The approximate distance is indicated at the top of the page, before the directions.

PRICE INDICATION
Next to the address and contact details of each location, we give an idea of how much you can expect to spend there. Unless otherwise stated, the amount given in restaurant listings is the average price of a main course. For sights and attractions, we indicate the cost of a regular full-price ticket.

GOOD TO KNOW
Most stores are open from Monday to Saturday until 8pm, but there are exceptions. In the former West Berlin, smaller shops can close as early as 2pm, although 4pm is more common.

LEGEND

● >> SIGHTS & ATTRACTIONS   ● >> FOOD & DRINK
● >> SHOPPING   ● >> MORE TO EXPLORE

Restaurants are often open all day and some keep their kitchens open until far after midnight. It's a myth that the only proper meal you can get in Berlin is Schnitzel and Bratwurst (thankfully!). There is an ever-growing number of top restaurants in this beautiful city. Very typical are the many *Frühstück-cafés* (breakfast joints) where they serve a hearty breakfast—in some cases until as late as 5pm. Weekends are made for brunch—preferably with a glass of *Sekt* (sparkling wine) on the side. Berliners love organic food and farmers markets. Especially in the eastern part, such as Mitte and Prenzlauer Berg, you'll stumble across a plethora of organic supermarkets and health-food stores. Vegetarian and vegan restaurants are popping up left, right, and center.

Don't worry too much about tipping—it's not customary, but it is appreciated (5 to 10 percent is normal). And don't forget—there are many places that do not accept credit cards!

Berlin has a smoking ban in bars and restaurants, although it's not strictly enforced. The rule of thumb: In smaller places it's usually okay to smoke if they don't serve food. Larger venues are more commonly smoke-free environments.

TYPICAL BERLIN

Although the Wall fell over 25 years ago (called *Die Wende*, or "turnaround"), Berlin is still not a city united. West is West, and East remains East. It also lacks a real city center. Instead, each district has its own little neighborhoods, called *Kiez*.

The numbering of houses is rather unique and something even the most seasoned visitor to Berlin can't really wrap their head around. Instead of using steadily increasing even and uneven numbers, the city uses a so-called "horse-

---

TUNED IN TO BERLIN!

GO TO WWW.TIMETOMOMO.COM FOR THE LATEST TIPS
NEW ADDRESSES + UP-AND-COMING NEIGHBORHOODS
+ POP-UP STORES + CONCERTS + FESTIVALS + MUCH MORE

shoe" system that stems from Prussia. This means that number 10 can be opposite number 220. There are small signs under the street names that indicate which numbers are in a particular block.

Most people who grew up in the former West side of the city speak good English, but people from the East (especially those over 40) grew up learning Russian as a second language.

May 1st is Labor Day, which in the Kreuzberg neighborhood is traditionally celebrated with demonstrations, notably around Kottbusser Tor.

PUBLIC HOLIDAYS

There are quite a number of German public holidays you want to take into account. On these days most shops and markets are closed and opening hours for certain sights will be different. In addition to religious holidays, like *Karfreitag* (Good Friday), *Ostermontag* (Easter Monday), *Christi Himmelfahrt* (Ascension Day), *Pfingsten* (Pentecost), and *Weihnachten* (Christmas Eve, Christmas Day, and Boxing Day), Germany observes the following public holidays:

January 1 > New Year's Day
May 1 > Labor Day
October 3 > *Tag der Deutschen Einheit* (German Unity Day)

HAVE ANY TIPS?

Shops and restaurants in Berlin come and go fairly regularly. We do our best to keep the walks and contact details as up to date as possible, and this is reflected in our digital products. We also do our best to update the print edition as often as we can. However, if despite our best efforts there is a place that you can't find or if you have any other comments or tips about this book, please let us know. Email info@momedia.nl, or leave a message on
www.timetomomo.com.

TRANSPORTATION

Berlin has two **airports:** Schönefeld and Tegel. The somewhat-controversial new airport, Berlin Brandenburg International, is scheduled to open its doors in 2018, after which the other two will probably be closed. You can take public transport from both airports to the city center. From Tegel you can catch a **JetExpress bus:** Line X9 goes to Bahnhof Zoo (15 minutes) and line TXL goes to Alexanderplatz (20 minutes). From Schönefeld, which is located outside the city, the S-Bahn light-rail line S9 will take you to the center of town in 40 minutes. There's also the **Airport Express** train that will get you there in half an hour. A taxi from Tegel to Mitte costs about €20, while a taxi from Schönefeld to Mitte will set you back at least twice that.

International **trains** arrive at Berlin Hauptbahnhof. S-Bahn lines S5, S7, and S75 connect this central station with all important stops in the city.

If you're renting a **car** in Berlin, remember to ask the rental company if the environmental sticker *(Umweltplakette)* is included on your car. This special sticker is needed to drive in the city's "green zones." You can also buy them at most gas stations for €5-10.

PUBLIC TRANSPORT

Public transport in Berlin is extensive and easy to navigate. There are **trams, buses,** and two types of **trains** (U-Bahn and S-Bahn). In the back of this guide you'll find a map with all the U- and S-Bahn lines. If you want to travel inside the center, you're best off buying a Berlin AB-ticket for €2.70. When you want to go to Schönefeld or Potsdam you'll need an ABC-ticket. It's valid for two hours for all types of public transport, but only as a single ride. You have to buy a new ticket for your return. Don't forget to stamp your ticket. If you're only traveling a short distance, buy a *Kurzstrecke* (€1.60)—it takes you a maximum of six bus or tram stops or three U- or S-Bahn stops. You can also buy a day ticket (€6.90) or one of the WelcomeCards: 48 hours (€19.50 for zones A and B), 72 hours (€26.70) or 5 days (€34.50). A WelcomeCard comes with a booklet with discount coupons for different sights. The tram, U-Bahn, and S-Bahn operate until around 12:30am. On the weekend, some U- and S-Bahns operate all night. There's also a network of **night buses** (with the letter N on the front) that covers the entire city. For more information on tickets, prices, and availability, go to *www.bvg.de*.

TAXIS

Taxis in Berlin are affordable and luggage is free of charge. If you're traveling with small children, let the driver know beforehand—they are not allowed to take young kids if they're not in a car seat. Berlin has many taxi stands, but you can also hail one on the street or call one. Three useful numbers are: Würfelfunk, t: 030210101; TaxiFunk, t: 030443322; and Taxi Quality, t: 030263000.

BIKING

Biking in Berlin is not just easy—it's fun. Berlin is becoming increasingly more **bike-friendly.** Keep in mind that many Berliners bike fast and don't always follow the rules. Most bikers wear a helmet, but it's not mandatory. Don't bike side-by-side with your buddies—cars don't appreciate it, and it's downright dangerous. Cars adhere strictly to the priority rules and so do bikers.

So yes—rent a bike! The walks through Mitte, Charlottenburg, and Schöneberg are great bike routes. You could also bike part of the Berliner Mauerweg (100 miles over the old border)—it's stunning. Or bike out of town via the Radfernweg Berlin-Usedom, Berlin-Kopenhagen, or part of the Wannseeroute. You can take the S-Bahn back to town, although you need to buy a special ticket for your bike.

Rental bikes from the German railway company (Deutsche Bahn, or DB) are installed at 80 locations in Mitte, Prenzlauer Berg, and Kreuzberg (Call a Bike, *www.callabike-interaktiv.de).* You have to register beforehand on their website or at the location for a one-time fee of €3. After that you can bike the entire city for €1 per half hour or a maximum of €15 per day. You could also go to one of the numerous bike-rental places, like Fahrradstation *(www.fahrradstation.com),* which has seven locations throughout the city.

Don't want to bike? Tour around on the bus. **City bus line 100** is much more fun than a touristy double-decker and takes you past all the major sights of Berlin.

1 The best Currywurst in the West can be found at **Curry 36.** > p. 109

2 The best Currywurst in the East is at **Konnopke's Imbiss.** > p. 46

3 **Mustafa's Gemüse Kebap** is well worth the wait. > p. 110

4 Grab a burrito on the go at **No Hablo Español.** > p. 66

5 The food trucks from **Bite Club Berlin** are a treat in the summer. > Eichenstrasse 4

6 Look for oysters, sausages, and subs at **Kollwitzmarkt.** > p. 57

7 Street Food Thursday in the **Markthalle Neun.** > p. 109

8 You'll find grilled Korean snacks at **Mmaah.** > p. 134

9 Try the Japanese hamburgers at **Shiso Burger.** > p. 35

10 The **Thaiwiese** in Preussen Park is a great spot for an Asian picnic. > Konstanzer Strasse 46

TOP 10 | RESTAURANTS

1 For DJs and movie nights, go to **Twinpigs.** > Boddinstrasse 57a

2 Try some old-school dancing at **Clärchens Ballhaus.** > p. 37

3 **Berghain** is quintessentially Berlin. > Rüdersdorfer Strasse 7

4 **Prince Charles** is an uber-cool club. > Prinzenstrasse 85F

5 Take pictures from the roof at the **House of Weekend club.** > Alexanderplatz 7

6 Party in old warehouses at **RAW-tempel.** > p. 74

7 Cocktails with a view at **Monkey Bar.** > p. 86

8 **Hops & Barley** serves Berlin brews. > p. 65

9 **Club Salon zur wilden Renate** feels like a theatrical house party. > Alt Stralau 70

10 Dance on the river at **Club der Visionäre.** > Am Flutgraben 1

TOP 10 | SUNDAY

1 Find vintage, art, and food at the **Mauerpark** on Sundays. > p. 42

2 Start your day as an Early Bird in the **Fernsehturm.** > p. 22

3 Take the S-Bahn into nature at the **Schlachtensee.** > p. 138

4 Browse the flea market at **Boxhagener Platz.** > p. 74

5 Climb the **Teufelsberg** and enjoy the view. > p. 138

6 **Go dancing** at an open-air party In the summertime. Check our website for info.

7 The **Flohmarkt on Arkonaplatz** has vintage treasures. > p. 54

8 Play ping pong in a park or on **Starplatz.** > p. 54

9 Spend the afternoon relaxing on **Tempelhofer Freiheit.** > p. 133

10 Do as the Berliners do: Sleep in and have a **late breakfast.**

WALK **1**

MITTE

ABOUT THE WALK

This walk takes you past all of Berlin's most iconic sights, as well as some great restaurants, coffee bars, and shops. The focus of this walk, however, is arts and culture. Don't be afraid to stray from the main route: There are plenty of side streets with interesting things to discover as well. Plan an entire day for this route, which can also be combined with Walk 2.

THE NEIGHBORHOODS

Berlin is often regarded as the most creative city in Europe, and if there's one district to which it owes this name, it's Mitte. Cultural life thrives here, especially in the **Scheunenviertel,** the former Jewish quarter just north of the river Spree. **Auguststrasse** and **Linienstrasse** is rapidly becoming an international art center with various galleries, **Mulackstrasse** and **Torstrasse** have many young and up-and-coming designers and creative businesses, and the area between **Invalidenstrasse** and Torstrasse is becoming increasingly more interesting. The hip cafés and restaurants dotted around the entire neighborhood also give the area a lively feel.

South of the Spree you'll find an area known for international business corporations, opulent shopping, and the government center (Regierungsviertel) with the famous boulevard **Unter den Linden.** For luxury and famous fashion brands, go to **Friedrichstrasse,** where you'll also find many notable Berlin attractions and sights nearby, such as **Checkpoint Charlie, Potsdamer Platz,** and the **Holocaust Memorial.** Part of Mitte's popularity amongst tourists is because the neighborhood, with places like the **Hackesche Höfe** and the **Gendarmenmarkt,** has an authentic and classic feel.

Germany's 20th-century history is palpable in the Mitte neighborhood. While traces of World Wars I and II remain, more recent history looms here as well, from **Alexanderplatz**—the former center of East Berlin—to the symbols of united Berlin: The **Brandenburger Tor** and the **Fernsehturm.** You'll also find Germany's most important art museums in Mitte on **Museumsinsel.**

SHORT ON TIME? HERE ARE THE HIGHLIGHTS
+ BRANDENBURGER TOR + FERNSEHTURM + REICHSTAG
+ TOPOGRAFIE DES TERRORS + CHECKPOINT CHARLIE

TIPS
// Must-do for first-time
visitors to Berlin
// Great for Sundays because
of the many museums
// Long walk, but also
bikeable

MITTE

WALK 1 DESCRIPTION (approx. 6.1 miles)

Start at the Gedenkstätte Berliner Mauer (Berlin Wall Memorial) **❶**. Head down the paths on the west or east side, or alternate between the two. Turn right down Brunnenstrasse **❷**, with its galleries and shops, and take a little break at Joris **❸**. Head to the intersection with Invalidenstrasse. Turn right for some culinary shopping **❹**, or continue the route, passing the book store **❺**, until you reach Torstrasse **❻**. Cross and take a left past Sankt Oberholz **❼**. Take the second right, Alte Schönhauser Strasse **❽**, and a left after the playground, onto Schendelgasse. Take in the renovated Plattenbau. At Almstadtstrasse, turn right and then left onto Hirtenstrasse. For the most magnificent view of the Volksbühne **❾**, look left. Continue down the road and turn right onto Rosa-Luxemburg-Strasse **❿**. Go right at the intersection. You can stop for lunch at Oliv **⓫** or go shopping on Münzstrasse **⓬**. If you want to see Alexanderplatz **⓭** and the Fernsehturm **⓮**, walk back in the direction of Karl-Liebknecht-Strasse. The route continues with a left turn and straight through Rochstrasse, underneath the train tracks and through Anna-Louisa-Karsch-Strasse towards Museumsinsel **⓯ ⓰**. Turn left onto Hinter dem Giesshaus and go right so you end up at Unter den Linden. At Friedrichstrasse turn right for some cultural shopping **⓱**, or go left **⓲**. Turn left again at Französische Strasse and immediately right into Gendarmenmarkt **⓳**. Walk on to Charlottenstrasse, turn right through Kronenstrasse, and head back to Friedrichstrasse and Checkpoint Charlie **⓴**. A bit further on is a nice place for coffee **㉑**. Walk through Zimmerstrasse in the direction of Topographie des Terrors **㉒**. The adjacent museum **㉓** is beautiful. At the end, turn right onto Potsdamer Platz **㉔** and follow the road towards the Holocaust Memorial **㉕**. Walk on to Brandenburger Tor **㉖** and after a slight turn you'll end up at the Reichstag building **㉗**. Walk to the water and turn right. Just after the rail bridge is a museum **㉘**. You've returned to Friedrichstrasse: Cross the road, go over the bridge, and turn right over the terrace. Walk along the Spree. Turn left after the Monbijoupark **㉙**, and left again after the Neue Synagoge **㉚**. Turn right onto Tucholskystrasse. Take a breather on the corner **㉛** before turning right onto Auguststrasse **㉜** for good food **㉝**, dancing **㉞**, and magazines **㉟**. At Grosse Hamburger Strasse turn right and cross diagonally to Sophienstrasse. At the end, take a right to reach Hackesche Höfe **㊱**.

SIGHTS & ATTRACTIONS

① The **Gedenkstätte Berliner Mauer** (Berlin Wall Memorial) is a telling monument that shows the impact the Wall had on life in Berlin. Approximately 720 feet of original wall remains, including a watch tower. Visit the memorial and don't forget to go inside S-Bahn station Nordbahnhof. When East Germany was known as the German Democratic Republic (GDR) this was a so-called ghost (closed) station.

bernauer strasse 111/119, www.berliner-mauer-gedenkstaette.de, u-bahn u8 bernauer strasse, s-bahn nordbahnhof

⑬ During the GDR era, **Alexanderplatz** was East Berlin's main square. The buildings and their surroundings still have a typical East German feel, like Galeria Kaufhof—once home to department store Centrum, a major retail store in East Berlin. The largest demonstration against the GDR regime took place right here in the fall of 1989. After the department store was renovated and shopping mall Alexa opened its doors, the square got its original role back as shopping center of the east. The **Weltzeituhr** (World Clock) shows the time in different world cities and is a very popular attraction.

alexanderplatz, s-bahn, u-bahn u2, u5, u8 alexanderplatz

⑭ Brandenburger Tor is not the only symbol of united Berlin—the **Fernsehturm** (Television Tower) is as well. It's the highest building in Berlin (at 1,208 feet) and a great landmark. Take the elevator to the visitor platform or the panoramic floor (666 feet high) and enjoy the view.

alexanderplatz, panoramastrasse 1a, www.tv-turm.de, t: 030247575875, open daily mar-oct 9am-midnight, nov-feb 10am-midnight, entrance €13, s-bahn, u-bahn u2, u5, u8 alexanderplatz

⑮ The **Museumsinsel** in the middle of the Spree is home to some of Germany's most important museums. The **Altes Museum** shows pieces from Classical antiquity, the **Alte Nationalgalerie** offers a look at 19th-century paintings, and the **Bode Museum** proudly displays a large sculpture collection. The **Pergamon Museum** houses archaeological treasures from the Middle East and the **Neues Museum** has Egyptian art. The island is also home to the **Berliner**

1961

Dom (Berlin Cathedral). On the other side of the water the newly-built **Berliner Stadtschloss** rises up above the skyline.
bodestrasse 1-3, www.smb.museum, t: 030266424242, see website for times and prices, s-bahn, u-bahn u6 friedrichstrasse

⑯ The **Deutsches Historisches Museum** (German Historical Museum, DHM) is located just outside of the Museumsinsel. The permanent exhibition is housed in the famous Unter den Linden building. In the newly-built, modern annex are temporary exhibits on the more current history of Germany. Tip: The lines at the Hinter dem Giesshaus entrance are significantly shorter.
unter den linden 2, www.dhm.de, t: 03020304, open daily 10am-6pm, entrance €8, s-bahn, u-bahn u6 friedrichstrasse

⑲ The **Gendarmenmarkt,** with its romantic architecture and two domed churches, is undoubtedly one of the most beautiful squares in Berlin. In the summer there are open-air concerts in front of the Konzerthaus, and there is a Christmas market in the winter.
gendarmenmarkt, u-bahn u2 stadtmitte, u6 französische strasse

⑳ On August 13, 1961 East German soldiers started building the Wall. The **Checkpoint Charlie** Museum at the crossing point between East and West Berlin tells the stories of often-unsuccessful attempts to escape. There's also a replica of the original guardhouse.
friedrichstrasse 43-45, www.mauer-museum.de, t: 0302537250, open daily 9am-10pm, entrance €12.50, u-bahn u6 kochstrasse

㉒ **Topographie des Terrors** is situated right where the SS and Gestapo conceived their cruellest methods for the oppression and persecution of their political opponents. This exhibition is the right place to refresh your historical consciousness before you continue on in this part of Berlin that is laden with Nazi history.
niederkirchnerstrasse 8, www.topographie.de, t: 03025450950, open daily 10am-8pm, free entrance, s-bahn, u-bahn u2 potsdamer platz, u6 kochstrasse

㉓ Museum **Martin-Gropius-Bau** is often described as one of Germany's most beautiful historic exhibition buildings. It was nearly destroyed during World War

II, and didn't reopen until 1981. The exhibitions are sensational and the topic of much conversation. Many artists, such as Ai Weiwei and Anish Kapoor, create pieces especially for the space. Avoid the long lines by booking tickets online.
niederkirchnerstrasse 7, www.berlinerfestspiele.de/gropiusbau, t: 030254860, open wed-mon 10am-7pm, hours may differ—check website, entrance €10 (varies), s-bahn, u-bahn u2 potsdamer platz

(24) In the 1920s **Potsdamer Platz** was alive and vibrant and the symbol of modern Berlin. All of that changed during the Cold War, when this place became a sad and desolate wasteland, stuck between East and West. Nowadays the square is once again flanked by cutting-edge architecture.
potsdamer platz, s-bahn, u-bahn u2 potsdamer platz

(25) The **Holocaust Memorial** consists of 2,711 concrete slabs commemorating the Jewish victims of World World II. You'd think this place would silence everyone who visits it, but people react very differently. And that was exactly what architect Peter Eisenman had in mind—to not tell the public how to react, but rather to let it happen naturally.
cora-berliner-strasse 1, www.stiftung-denkmal.de, t: 0302007660, open visitors center apr-sep tue-sun 10am-8pm, oct-mar tue-sun 10am-7pm, free entrance, s-bahn brandenburger tor

(26) **Brandenburger Tor** (Brandenburg Gate) was built in 1791 based on Greek design. It's the only remaining gate of a wall that once surrounded the city of Berlin. Located on Pariser Platz, it's flanked by embassies and the prestigious Hotel Adlon. Before the Wall fell, the lonely gate symbolized the separation of the city, but nowadays it's seen as a triumphal arch and a symbol of German unity. It was here that Ronald Reagan spoke his legendary words: "Mr. Gorbachev, tear down this wall!"
ebertstrasse / corner unter den linden, s-bahn brandenburger tor

(27) The **Reichstag building** is where parliament resides. Walk up to the glass dome, designed by architect Sir Norman Foster, and up to the roof through an ingenious spiral construction. The views are spectacular. When you're there, have a look in Parliament Hall. For security reasons you have to book an entry

time at least two business days in advance. Tip: Combine your visit with dinner at Käfer Dachgarten Restaurant *(www.feinkost-kaefer.de)*.

platz der republik 1, www.bundestag.de, open daily 8am-midnight, restaurant 9am-4:30pm & 6:30pm-midnight, free entrance, s-bahn brandenburger tor, u-bahn u55 bundestag

㉘ There are few places in Berlin where the impact of the Wall is more poignant than at the permanent exhibition *Grenz Erfahrungen* in the **Tränenpalast** (Palace of Tears). During the GDR era this was the train station where people would bid farewell to their loved ones after a visit. Countless tears were shed here—tears of anger, of hopelessness, and of grief. On display are photographs, artifacts, and eyewitness stories.

reichstagufer 17, www.hdg.de/berlin/traenenpalast, t: 030467777911, open tue-fri 9am-7pm, sat-sun & holidays 10am-6pm, free entrance, s-bahn, u-bahn u6 friedrichstrasse

㉚ The golden dome of the **Neue Synagoge** (built in 1866) was the pride and joy of the Jewish community in Berlin. The building survived the Kristallnacht (Night of Broken Glass) in 1938, but it was destroyed during a bomb raid in 1943. The synagogue was rebuilt and now houses a permanent exhibition on Jewish life in Berlin.

oranienburger strasse 28-30, www.centrumjudaicum.de, t: 03088028300, open apr-sep sun-fri 10am-6pm, oct-mar sun-thu 10am-6pm, fri 10am-3pm, price museum €5, dome €5, s-bahn oranienburgerstrasse, u-bahn u6 oranienburger tor

㊱ In the Roaring '20s the **Hackesche Höfe,** filled with restaurants and dance halls, was the beating heart of Berlin. After *Die Wende* (the turnaround) this Jugendstil complex was restored and the eight interconnected courtyards are now a magnet for tourists. Because people still live on the upper floors of the buildings, the courtyards are quiet at night. There are a few bars and restaurants and one large cinema in the first and second courtyards.

sophienstrasse 6, www.hackesche-hoefe.de, t: 03028098010, open daily until 10pm, courtyard I and II always open, free entrance, s-bahn hackescher markt, u-bahn u8 weinmeisterstrasse

FOOD & DRINK

③ It's all about soups and salads at **Joris,** plus baked potatoes loaded with what-ever you like. They serve up a lovely warm lunch. Go to the bar, place your order, and find a table in the back or on the sidewalk outside. They also have a nice selection of sweets. The place tends to get busy, but take that as a good sign.
brunnenstrasse 158, www.joris-berlin.de, t: 03047365973, open mon-fri 9am-5pm, price lunch €6, u-bahn u8 bernauer strasse

⑦ **Sankt Oberholz** was once a beer hall and hamburger joint. Now it's where freelancers with their laptops go to work. Many a Berlin startup was dreamt up right here. With self-service coffee, juice, and sandwiches, it's no wonder this place is so popular. The one downside is that it's hard to find a free table.
rosenthaler strasse 72a, www.sanktoberholz.de, t: 03024085586, open mon-thu 8am-midnight, fri 8am-3am, sat 9am-3am, sun 9am-midnight, price €4, u-bahn u8 rosenthaler platz

⑧ Nowadays bakers that bake their own bread are, unfortunately, rather rare. **Zeit für Brot,** however, is an exception to the rule. They bake their own bread on the premises all day long. With tables both inside and outside, you can have breakfast until well in the afternoon. Indulge in a coffee with *Zimtschnecke*—a lovely soft cinnamon bun—or a piece of *Streuselkuchen* (crumble cake).
alte schönhauser strasse 4, www.zeitfuerbrot.com, t: 03028046780, open mon-fri 7:30am-8pm, sat 8am-8pm, sun 8am-6pm, price €4, u-bahn u2 rosa-luxemburg-platz

⑪ **Oliv** is a popular place, and rightfully so. They serve delicious quiches and breakfasts (amongst other offerings). Want to do some people watching? Their outdoor seating area is the perfect place. The decor is effectively simple with wooden tables and stools, and always one prominent piece of art on the wall.
münzstrasse 8, www.oliv-cafe.de, t: 03089206540, open mon-fri 8:30am-7pm, sat 9:30am-7pm, sun 10am-6pm, price €6, u-bahn u8 weinmeisterstrasse

⑱ **Cookies Cream** is the best vegetarian restaurant in Berlin, and even getting there is an experience. You'll follow an almost surrealistic route along the dumpsters of a hotel and a gigantic chandelier. Ring the doorbell underneath

SUPPE	SALATE	OFENKARTOFFEL
= 4,50	+ + = 6.-	+ [DIP] = 4,50
EXTRAS	+ + = 7,50	+ [DIP] + = 6.-
= 1,50	joris-klassiker = 7,50	+ [HOT] = 6.-
+ = 1,50	salat des tages = 6,50	+ [HOT] + = 7,50

the light bulbs, walk up the stairs—it's above Club Cookies—and enjoy a laid-back dinner.

behrenstrasse 55, between westin grand hotel and komische oper, www.cookiescream.de, t: 03027492940, open tue-sat starting 6pm, price three course menu €39, u-bahn u6 französische strasse, s-bahn brandenburger tor

㉑ Beautiful decor, good coffee, scrumptious subs and mouth-watering cake sums up **Westberlin.** They have a large selection of magazines and even a few souvenirs.

215, www.westberlin-bar-shop.de, t: 03025922745, open mon-fri 8:30am-7pm, sat-sun 10am-7pm, price €5, u-bahn u6 kochstrasse

㉛ With only French toast, Weisswurst, and Weizenbier, **Keyser Soze**'s menu is deceptively simple—a concept that might even apply to the entire place. It's always busy, always has a good vibe, and always has the sound of the U-Bahn that runs underneath.

tucholskystrasse 33, www.keyser-soze.de, t: 03028599489, open daily 7:30am-3am, price €10, u-bahn u6 oranienburger tor, s-bahn oranienburger strasse

㉝ Berlin's first Jewish girls' school, the **Ehemalige Jüdische Mädchenschule,** has a turbulent history. The building was completely derelict, but is now reno-vated and a great place to eat and drink. Pauly Saal is a very good restaurant, reminiscent of the 1920s. Mogg, on the other side, offers a variety of delcious Jewish delicatessen, such as a pastrami sandwiches and matzo-ball soup. The building is also home to a few galleries and Museum The Kennedys.

auguststrasse 11-13, www.maedchenschule.org, see website for times and prices, u-bahn u6 oranienburger tor, s-bahn oranienburgerstrasse

SHOPPING

② **Brunnenstrasse** is a long street lined with galleries, shops, and great places for coffee or lunch. One place you don't want to miss is Objets Trouvés (nr. 169). On the corner of Invalidenstrasse (at #19-21), you'll find the former Kaufhaus Jandorf just across from the beautiful Weinbergspark. Toward the Rosenthaler

Strasse is a facade with the text: *"Dieses Haus stand früher in einem anderen Land"* –"This house used to be in a different country."
brunnenstrasse, u-bahn u8 bernauer strasse, rosenthaler platz

④ The first part of **Invalidenstrasse** recently welcomed a host of new places to eat, like Tommi's Burger Joint and the Israeli Dyimalaya. A bit further down the street is the fantastic delicatessen Vom Einfachen das Gute. Or grab some snacks at the Ackerhalle (the former Markthalle VI), which is now a supermarket.
invalidenstrasse, u-bahn u8 rosenthaler platz

⑤ **Ocelot** is a stunning book store: beautifully decorated with long tables and hundreds of books. Their staff is knowledgeable and always happy to help. There are places to sit throughout the store, and a huge reading table where you can sit with a coffee. They have many books on Berlin, but mostly sell literature.
brunnenstrasse 181, www.ocelot.de, t: 03097894592, open mon-sat 10am-8pm, u-bahn u8 rosenthaler platz

⑥ **Torstrasse** deserves a chapter of its own: This 1.2-mile-long street is getting more fun every year. Yes, there's traffic and it's busy, but it has some great restaurants (try 3 Minutes sur Mer at #167 or Noto at #173), galleries, and stunning shops (check out Happy Shop at #67 and Stue at #70).
torstrasse, u-bahn u8 rosenthaler platz, u2 rosa-luxemburg-platz

⑩ On **Rosa-Luxemburg-Strasse** you'll find small shops with big surprises. Lovers of all things paper should indulge at Luiban (#28), while Type Hype (#9) sells accessories featuring letters of the alphabet. Ulf Haines Men (#26) sells men's clothing and Ulf Haines Women (#9) offers women's fashion. Go to Blush (#22) for lingerie.
rosa-luxemburg-strasse, open mon-sat noon-8pm, u-bahn u2 rosa-luxemburg-platz

⑫ **Münzstrasse** and **Alte Schönhauser Strasse** are great for shopping, but don't forget to explore surrounding streets like Mulackstrasse, Rochstrasse and Weinmeisterstrasse, with everything from flagship stores to vintage boutiques.
münzstrasse/alte schönhauser strasse, most stores open mon-sat noon-8pm, u-bahn u8 weinmeisterstrasse

㉗ Even if you don't read German books, **Dussmann das Kulturkaufhaus** is well worth a visit. It's a gigantic book store with four floors, each with several sections. The ground floor is home to paper and stationary, sheet music, and English books. Next to the main entrance you can buy tickets for concerts and theater productions. The store is also home to a spectacular 2,900-square foot vertical garden, with over 6,000 tropical plants.

friedrichstrasse 90, www.kulturkaufhaus.de, t: 03020251111, open mon-fri 9am-midnight, sat 9am-11:30pm, s-bahn, u-bahn u6 friedrichstrasse

㉜ **Auguststrasse** was once the center of the Jewish community, but now it's where the Berlin Biënnale for Contemporary Art takes place. Pop into small venues like the Kunst-Werke gallery and interior-design shop Marron Hay Berlin. Feeling hungry? Try Shiso Burger, Simon, or Strandbad Mitte. Hackbarth's is a great place for a beer at night.

augustrasse, u-bahn u6 oranienburger tor, u8 weinmeisterstrasse, s-bahn oranienburger strasse

㉟ Inspiration is guaranteed in **Do you read me?!**. This shop sells magazines and books from at least 20 different countries about art, fashion, photography, design, architecture, music, and more.

auguststrasse 28, www.doyoureadme.de, t: 03069549695, open mon-sat 10am-7:30pm, s-bahn oranienburger strasse

MORE TO EXPLORE

⑨ The **Volksbühne** is a theater for and by the people. It's an impressive building dating back to 1913-1914 and was completely renovated during the 1950s. The beautiful entrance and foyers alone make this building well worth a visit. If you don't speak German, get tickets for *Murmel Murmel;* it's the only word used during the 80-minute show.

rosa-luxemburg-platz, www.volksbuehne-berlin.de, t: 03024065777, entrance approx. €20, u-bahn u2 rosa-luxemburg-platz

㉙ The Rococo Schloss Monbijou palace used to be located here in **Monbijou-park,** but it didn't survive World Word II or the GDR era. The park was a construction site until the early 21st century, when it was transformed into a public park with an open-air swimming pool, playground, theater, restaurant, and lounge chairs along the Spree. On a warm summer night, go to beach bar Mitte on the Spree, where they dance tango and salsa.

oranienburger strasse, t: 0303339509, s-bahn oranienburger strasse

㉞ Tea dance, cha-cha-cha, and the waltz: It may sound old-fashioned, but every Sunday afternoon hipster *Jungs* (youths) go dancing in **Clärchens Ballhaus.** This '50s dance hall is open almost every night. Drink a beer in the front yard or, on Sundays, enjoy a piano concert or a lecture about the Ballhaus in the Mirror Hall. Clärchens also offers food. If you fancy one of their famous *Berliner Buletten* (German burgers), but not the Friday-night rush, go to the small bistro Altes Europa at Gipsstrasse 11—it's part of Clärchens.

auguststrasse 24, www.ballhaus.de, t: 0302829295, open daily from 11am, from noon in winter, price €10, s-bahn oranienburger strasse, u-bahn u6 oranienburger tor

WALK **2**

PRENZLAUER BERG

ABOUT THE WALK

The walk starts in an area that is officially still part of Mitte: At the bottom of the hill that gave the neighborhood its name (*"Berg"* means mountain). You'll walk past squares and through interesting streets on this side of the Prenzlauer Allee thoroughfare. On the other side you'll find the nice Botzöw-viertel neighborhood, bordering the urban green of Volkspark Friedrichshain.

THE NEIGHBORHOODS

Prenzlauer Berg was once one of the poorest and most densely populated neighborhoods in Berlin. This **old workers' district,** with beautiful houses from around 1900, withstood World War II remarkably well. During the GDR years this part of the city was neglected, and artists used the grey tenements as their sanctuary. The rebellion against the GDR regime started in this part of the city, and if you visit **Gethsemanekirche** and **Zionskirche,** you'll learn a lot about that era.

After the Wall fell, Prenzlauer Berg—with its telling nickname "The Wild East"— became the most exciting part of Berlin. Thanks to its central location and alternative vibe, many unique stores, trendy bars, and restaurants set up shop. These days, the rebels of yesteryear have been replaced by couples pushing strollers, which gives Prenzlauer Berg the reputation of being the most fertile neighborhood in Berlin. But something of its previous vibrancy remains, and now this is the place to be for foodies and lovers of life. You'll find the best *Kaffee und Kuchen* (coffee and cake) and **Sunday brunch** that Berlin has to offer.

The southern part of Prenzlauer Berg is still somewhat anarchistic, but there are fewer squatters occupying the buildings. The long Kastanienallee is called the "casting alley" for a reason—the street has a reputation for providing both a great cinematographic backdrop, and for the photogenic faces that can be spotted walking around. **Kollwitzplatz** and its surroundings, a place that used to be home to many artists, now is home to yuppies and so-called *Schwaben* (rich Germans from the Stuttgart area). Young families, Web entrepreneurs, and media figures dominate this part of town, which is littered with restaurants and shops. In the little community around **Helmholtzplatz** you'll find many cafés, restaurants, and a handful of shops that attract a young clientele. In the western part of Prenzlauer Berg is **Mauerpark,** the former border between East and West Berlin.

SHORT ON TIME? HERE ARE THE HIGHLIGHTS
+ MAUERPARK + ODERBERGER STRASSE + KOLLWITZPLATZ
+ ZIONSKIRCHE + HELMHOLZPLATZ

TIPS

// Interesting walk if you have visited Berlin before
// Great on a Sunday because of the many markets
// Cobbled streets are not so good for biking

PRENZLAUER BERG

1. Galão
2. Nola's
3. Glücklich am Park
4. Zionskirche / Zionskirchplatz
5. Arkonaplatz
6. Kastanienallee
7. Langbrett / Patagonia
8. Mazooka Store
9. Oderberger Straße
10. Prater Biergarten
11. Mauerpark
12. Linnen
13. Les Valseuses
14. Konnopke's Imbiß
15. Kulturbrauerei
16. Museum in der Kulturbrauerei
17. No Wodka
18. Osmans Töchter
19. Supalife Kiosk
20. YOnkel Ork
21. Gethsemane Church
22. Kontinentalwaren
23. Herr Nilsson Godis
24. Starplatz
25. Alois S.
26. Helmholtzplatz
27. Goldhahn & Sampson
28. Pomeranza Design Ranch
29. Anna Blume
30. November
31. Kollwitzplatz / Kollwitzmarkt
32. Wasserturmplatz
33. The Barn Roastery
34. Fleischerei

WALK 2 DESCRIPTION (approx. 4.7 miles)

Start at the bottom of the hill with a good breakfast **1** **2**. Then turn left onto Fehrbelliner Strasse. On the corner you can eat waffles or go clothes shopping **3**. Turn right onto Zionskirchstrasse **4**. A little bit further on is a great market **5**. Walk to Kastanienallee **6** and turn left. This street is bustling with fun little shops **7** **8**. Continue until you get to Oderberger Strasse **9** and take a left or, if you feel like a beer, walk just a little bit further **10**. At the end of Oderberger Strasse you'll find Mauerpark **11**. Turn right before the park for three places to eat **12** **13**—one of them underneath the train tracks **14**. Walk beneath the tracks. Take a right for some culture **15** **16** or go diagonally left and continue the walk through Pappelallee. Here you'll find many great shops **17** and a Turkish restaurant **18**. In a little side street is a shop that sells lithographs **19**. A bit further down Pappelallee is a store that sells all kinds of gadgets **20**. Turn left on Stargarder Strasse. The church **21** played a big part in the fall of the Wall. Walk around the church and back in the direction of Pappelallee. Continue straight on through the heart of the residential area. Buy something pretty at Kontinentalwaren **22** or get some sweets from Herr Nilsson Godis **23**, play table tennis **24**, or indulge in some tapas **25**. At the square, take a right onto Dunckerstrasse, towards Helmholtzplatz **26**. Here you'll have plenty of choices for lunch or dinner. You can also buy some snacks at the delicatessen **27**. Walk on until you reach Raumerstrasse and turn left. Go right after Pomeranza **28**, through Senefelderstrasse toward Danziger Strasse. Cross the street and go straight onto Kollwitzstrasse, where you'll find Anna Blume with its outdoor seating **29**. Take a right after the book tree through Sredzkistrasse. There's a restaurant on the corner **30**. Turn left to find the popular meeting place of the latte macchiato mamas: Kollwitzplatz **31**, where there's a farmers market twice a week. Turn left and then right onto Kollwitzstrasse. At Knaackstrasse, take a left past Wasserturmplatz **32**. Walk up or around the square, through Belforter Strasse, then right and immediately left. Walk until the end of Kollwitzstrasse, cross Metzer Strasse, and walk along the little park straight on down. On Schönhauser Allee you can have a coffee **33** or steak **34** just before you walk into Mitte.

SIGHTS & ATTRACTIONS

④ **Zionskirche** is where, in the 1930s, church-minister Bonhoeffer warned against Nazism, and where the religious revolt against the GDR regime began in the 1980s. You can find out all about its turbulent history inside. On Sundays you can climb the tower. **Zionskirchplatz** is home to many restaurants.

zionskirchplatz, www.zionskirche-berlin.de, open mon 8pm-10pm, tue & fri-sat 1pm-7pm, wed 4pm-7pm, sun noon-5pm, price tour €2, u-bahn u8 rosenthaler platz

⑪ **Mauerpark** is located on what used to be the border area between East and West. On Sunday the park fills up with a flea market, popular with tourists and Berliners alike. You can get a bite to eat from one of the many vendors, or listen to a cool band play. Sit on one of the swings on the small hill for a great view.

eberswalder strasse, www.mauerpark.info, u-bahn u2 eberswalder strasse

⑯ Daily life under communist dictatorship is the focus of the *"Alltag in der DDR"* exhibition in **Museum in der Kulturbrauerei.** Eyewitness stories alternate with some 8,000 items on display.

knaackstrasse 97, www.hdg.de/berlin/museum-in-der-kulturbrauerei/, t: 030467777911, open tue-wed & fri-sun 10am-6pm, thu 10am-8pm, free entrance, u-bahn u2 eberswalder strasse

㉑ **Gethsemane Church** was built at the end of the 19th century. The *Geistekämpfer* (spiritual fighter) statue by Ernst Barlach that stands in front of the facade commemorates the demonstrations of 1989, in which this church played a big role. There's an information kiosk on the other side of the street.

stargarder strasse 77, www.ekpn.de/kirchen/gethsemanekirche, open sun starting 11am, free entrance, s-bahn, u-bahn u2 schönhauser allee

㉜ On **Wasserturmplatz** you'll find a romantic park where once was a water reservoir. Things were not always this idyllic, though. In 1933 the Nazis used this area for their first concentration camp. Now you'll find benches, grapevines, and rose bushes here.

wasserturmplatz, between knaackstrasse and belforter strasse, u-bahn u2 senefelderplatz

FOOD & DRINK

(1) Coffeebar **Galão** is named after a Portuguese espresso that's served with warm milk foam. Try a *pastel de nata* or a croissant while standing at the window. They also have a few chairs at the door.

weinbergsweg 8, www.galao-berlin.de/cafe, t: 03044046882, open mon-fri 7:30am-8pm, sat 8am-8pm, sun 9am-9pm, price €4, u-bahn u8 rosenthaler platz

(2) **Nola's** is located at a small park on the Weinbergsweg. Everything in this café feels Swiss, from the chalet-type building and the lounge chairs out on the patio to the delicious Swiss dishes. On Sunday they serve up a mean breakfast.

veteranenstrasse 9, www.nola.de, t: 03044040766, open daily 10am-1am, price €14, u-bahn u8 rosenthaler platz

(10) The **Prater Biergarten** is one of the oldest restaurants in Prenzlauer Berg. There used to be a beer hall here, but nowadays Prater is part of the Volksbühne, an avant-garde theater. The beautiful yard is a great place to be on a summer night with a beer in hand and snacks like Bratwurst or an *Ofenkartoffel* (baked potato).

kastanienallee 7-9, www.pratergarten.de, t: 0304485688, open daily from noon apr-sep depending on the weather, €4, u-bahn u2 eberswalder strasse

(12) Delicious subs, a great breakfast, delectable cakes, or just a coffee with an authentic *Splitterbrötchen* (a typical sweet bun from Berlin) are what you'll find at **Linnen.** The café's interior is a mixture of modern and antique.

eberswalder strasse 35, www.linnenberlin.com, t: 03047372444, open mon 9am-noon, tue-sat 9am-4pm, sun 9am-6pm, price €6, u-bahn u2 eberswalder strasse

(13) At **Les Valseuses** a hip road bike adorns the wall and you sit on unfinished wood benches and classic bistro chairs. The two owners—one Belgian and the other French—have worked in a few famous Berlin restaurants. They serve up bistro dishes and unexpected aperitifs like the Diabolo.

eberswalder strasse 28, www.lesvalseuses.de, t: 03075522032, open daily starting 6:30pm, price €16, u-bahn u2 eberswalder strasse

⑭ **Konnopke's Imbiss** is world-famous because of its homemade *Currywurst* (sausage with a spicy tomato-based curry sauce), which is a typical Berlin delicacy. It's located under the train tracks and there's always a long line with everyone from construction workers to CEOs.

schönhauser allee 44b, www.konnopke-imbiss.de, t: 0304427765, open mon-fri 9am-8pm, sat 11:30am-8pm, price €1.90, u-bahn u2 eberswalder strasse

⑱ **Osmans Töchter** is one of the better Turkish restaurants in Berlin. It's a light and happy place that serves up modern cuisine from Istanbul on big platters to share. Making reservations is a good idea.

pappelallee 15, www.osmanstoechter.de, t: 03032663388, open daily 5:30pm-midnight, price €12, u-bahn u2 eberswalder strasse

㉕ **Alois S.** (named after writer Alois Senefelder and the street it's located on) is a cozy restaurant with a large outdoor seating area and playground. They serve tapas and simple Spanish entrées. Want to watch a soccer game? They show all important matches live on TV.

senefelder strasse 18, www.aloiss.de, t: 03044719680, open mon-sat 4pm-1am, sun 11am-2am (earlier in winter), price tapas €4, main course €10, s-bahn prenzlauer allee

㉖ In the afternoon, starting 3pm-ish, **Helmholtzplatz** fills up with parents and kids. In the middle of the square is a huge playground and the Kiezkind café, where kids can play in an indoor sandbox while their parents enjoy a *Milchkaffee* (coffee with milk). The square is lined with cute shops, bars, and restaurants. Walk around and take your pick. Try lunch at Liebling and a beer in Wohn-zimmer—a real Berlin-kinda place with furniture that looks like it came straight from the flea market. At night, have dinner just around the corner at Sasaya (Lychener Strasse 50), a quality Japanese restaurant. Two other favorites also opened their doors here: Café Sankt Oberholz and Victoria met Albert, which sells awesome home accessories and cool clothing. Don't miss VAL, where sustainability meets design in Scandinavian products.

helmholtzplatz, s-bahn prenzlauer allee, u-bahn u2 eberswalder strasse

㉙ Expect a full house at **Anna Blume,** because their breakfast is legendary. During the week you can make a reservation (recommended), but on weekends

it's first come, first served. Their three-tiered cake stand with breakfast bites is well worth the wait. Too late for breakfast? Go in the afternoon for *Kaffee mit Kuchen* (coffee with cake)—they have their own bakery.

kollwitzstrasse 83, www.cafe-anna-blume.de, t: 03044048749, open daily 8am-12am, price breakfast for two €18.50, u-bahn u2 eberswalder strasse

㉚ **November**'s menu is traditional food: simple but good. Try the *Königsberger Klopse* (meatballs with caper sauce) or *Senfeier* (eggs with mustard) with mashed potatoes. Their large patio is a great spot for people-watching.

husemannstrasse 15, www.cafe-november.de, t: 0304428425, open mon-fri from 6pm, sat-sun from 10am, price €13, u-bahn u2 eberswalder strasse

㉝ In coffeebar **The Barn Roastery** they keep their beans in close check—from crop to cup. Enjoy a cup with an excellent sub sandwich or delicious piece of cake. This is also a good place to get coffee equipment and filters. The Barn has another location at Auguststrasse 58.

schönhauser allee 8, www.thebarn.de, open mon-fri 8am-6pm, sat-sun 10am-6pm, price coffee €2.50, u-bahn u2 senefelderplatz

㉞ In Berlin they like to name their bars or restaurants after the words on the buildings. **Fleischerei,** once a butcher shop, is now a restaurant with a meaty menu. The food is good and the interior intimate and fresh.

schönhauser allee 8, www.fleischerei-berlin.com, t: 03050182117, open mon-fri noon-3pm & 6:30pm-midnight, sat-sun 6:30pm-midnight, price €16, u-bahn u2 senefelderplatz

SHOPPING

③ Concept store Kauf Dich Glücklich (Buy Yourself Happy) has a few locations, one of which is **Glücklich am Park** (Happy at the Park). On the ground floor they sell waffles and ice cream, and the second floor has trendy and affordable clothing. Other locations are on Oderberger Strasse and Rosenthaler Strasse.

kastanienallee 54, www.kaufdichgluecklich-shop.de, t: 03041725651, open daily 10am-8pm, u-bahn u8 rosenthaler platz

⑥ The **Kastanienallee** is sometimes called "casting alley." This place is all about seeing and being seen. There are many hip fashion stores (Tatchers at #21 for the girls, Fein und Ripp at #95 for the guys), great shoes (BQL at #75) and handy hat shops. Upcycling Deluxe at #22 only sells products made with recycled materials—very Berlin. There are also traditional souvenir shops (Heimat Berlin at #14 that sells beard products) and a squatters' café—in short, this is not a boring part of town. There are many places for a quick lunch, like Babel (at #33) with Lebanese specialties where you sit amongst big bunches of fresh flowers. W-Der Imbiss (#49) started out as a statement against the growing fast-food culture, and nowadays is an institution. Order a bowl of hot lentil soup or a delicious naan pizza.

kastanienallee, u-bahn u2 eberswalder strasse, u8 rosenthaler platz

⑦ "Surfers ride the waves, longboarders ride the street." **Langbrett** is a Berlin longboard label that also sells accessories and the edgy eco-friendly clothing made by **Patagonia.** Don't forget to browse through the small accessories at the checkout.

kastanienallee 44, www.langbrett.com, t: 03041997155, open mon-sat 11am-7pm, u-bahn u8 rosenthaler platz

⑧ Classic basics, their own label, T-shirts and sweaters, timeless fashion, and a number of vintage pieces are what you'll find at **Mazooka Store.** Quality and fair trade are key words here.

kastanienallee 34, www.mazooka.de, t: 03044044628, open mon-sat noon-7pm, u-bahn u8 rosenthaler strasse

⑨ **Oderberger Strasse** is a myriad of restaurants and shops. Paul's Boutique (#47) sells vintage sneakers and T-shirts; VEB Orange (#29) offers crockery, old maps, and stuff from the sixties and seventies; Teigwaren (#41) sells delicious ravioli; and for kids' clothing, visit HIT-IN TV (#34). At #35 you'll find Bonanza Coffee Heroes. Their beans are used by many good coffee places in Berlin and, of course, they use them for their own coffee as well—this is the real deal.

oderberger strasse, open mon-sat from around noon, u-bahn u2 eberswalder strasse

⑰ From Berlin, Poland is just around the corner—a country that is still rather unknown to many people. The beautifully decorated and light-and-airy **No Wodka** sells art and home accessories exclusively from Polish designers. The shop itself was devised by a design agency from Warsaw and changes all the time. They sell furniture, clothing, jewelry, and art.

pappelallee 10, www.nowodka.com, t: 03048623086, open mon-sat noon-7pm, u-bahn u2 eberswalder strasse

⑲ **Supalife Kiosk** is a gallery that displays work from young illustrators and urban artists. You'll see stunning screen prints, books, postcards, funny T-shirts, and calendars for sale. Artists can display their work for six weeks, after which new exhibits are displayed.

raumerstrasse 40, www.supalife.de, t: 03044678826, open thu-tue 11:30am-7:30pm, u-bahn u2 eberswalder strasse

⑳ Homemade rubber stamps, gifts, crib mobiles, postcards—you name it, **YOnkel Ork** sells it. This little shop is filled with beautiful accessories for the home and office.

pappelallee 63, www.yonkelork.de, t: 03021466241, open mon-sat 10am-6pm, u-bahn u2 eberswalder strasse, s-bahn or u-bahn u2 schönhauser allee

㉒ Everything at **Kontinentalwaren** is made in Europe. They have many German products, like *Klar-Seife* (soap), melamine, and egg cups. While the products are mostly household items, you'll also find toys and stationery.

stargarder strasse 19, www.kontinentalwaren.de, t: 03083218990, open mon-fri 11am-7:30pm, sat 11am-6pm, u-bahn u2 schönhauser allee

㉓ There are many Scandinavians in Berlin, and they even have their own candy store. **Herr Nilsson Godis** sells candy—and lots of it—from large containers and glass jars. Grab a bag or jar and fill it up with your favorites. There's another store in Friedrichshain (Wühlischstrasse 58).

stargarder strasse 58, www.herrnilsson.com, t: 03054594585, open mon-tue 11am-7pm, wed-fri 11am-8pm, sat noon-6pm, sun 1pm-6pm, s-bahn prenzlauer allee, u-bahn u2 schönhauser allee

㉗ **Goldhahn & Sampson** sells beautifully wrapped delicacies, artisan breads, chocolates, teas, coffees, and wines. They also organize cooking classes, and if you love cook books, browse through their selection—the largest in Berlin.
dunckerstrasse 9, www.goldhahnundsampson.de, open mon-fri 8am-8pm, sat 9am-8pm, s-bahn prenzlauer allee, u-bahn u2 eberswalder strasse

㉘ At **Pomeranza Design Ranch** you'll find accessories for your home, bags, postcards and prints, kitchen stuff, and kids' T-shirts with a print of the Fernsehturm. You can also get a coffee with something sweet and enjoy it outside on the sidewalk.
raumerstrasse 19, www.pomeranza-shop.de, t: 03048495760, open mon-fri 10am-7pm, sat 11am-6pm, s-bahn prenzlauer allee, u-bahn u2 eberswalder strasse

MORE TO EXPLORE

⑤ On Fridays there is a food market on **Arkonaplatz** where you can eat smoked fish or delicious Turkish snacks. The plaza has a great flea market on Sundays.
arkonaplatz, www.troedelmarkt-arkonaplatz.de, open fri noon-7pm, sun 10am-4pm, u-bahn u8 bernauer strasse

⑮ Long ago the buildings of the **Kulturbrauerei** were used to brew beer. Now this renovated brick building complex houses a cinema, several cafés, and a few clubs. In December they have a Scandinavian Christmas market. Alternate entrances are on Sredzkistrasse and Knaackstrasse.
schönhauser allee 36, www.kulturbrauerei.de, t: 030467777911, open daily from 10am, u-bahn u2 eberswalder strasse

㉔ **Starplatz** is a square like any other in Berlin, with benches under the trees and a few ping pong tables. A nearby store on Helmholtzplatz sells paddles and balls, so if you want to mingle with the locals, try your hand at a game. Or you can just sit and relax!
starplatz, hoek stargarder strasse / dunckerstrasse, s-bahn prenzlauer allee, u-bahn u2 schönhauser allee

ANTIQUE
ORIGINAL
Lithographs

㉛ After the Wall fell, the beautiful old houses that flank **Kollwitzplatz** were all restored and sold or rented at high prices. There are a number of restaurants lining the plaza, and the little park is a perfect spot to sit and relax. On Thursdays and Saturdays the **Kollwitzmarkt** offers delicious produce from organic farmers from out of town.

kollwitzplatz/kollwitzstrasse, market open thu noon-7pm, sat 9am-4pm, u-bahn u2 senefelderplatz

WALK **3**

FRIEDRICHSHAIN

ABOUT THE WALK

This walk is not that long, but if you like architecture, you can also start a bit farther back on Karl-Marx-Allee. That makes the first part of the route a lot longer, but it's an easy and quiet walk. The streets surrounding Boxhagener Platz are all interesting, so you can go off-route a little and wander around. RAW-tempel is especially great during the day.

THE NEIGHBORHOODS

Friedrichshain is the most authentic part of East Berlin, full of punk rockers, **graffiti,** and former East Germans. But it is also an area in flux, with many old properties being renovated and a steady stream of young families moving in.

Together, original residents and newcomers make Friedrichshain an area of interesting contrasts. This former blue-collar neighborhood constantly sees new creative enterprises popping up. Young fashion designers, artists, musicians, and students love to set up shop here. The vibe is alternative and raw. But its sharp edges are slowly softening—despite graffiti on the walls protesting the inevitable yuppification and left-wing political squatters who refuse to be silenced.

In the western part of the neighborhood you'll find **Karl-Marx-Allee,** flanked by impressive buildings like **Frankfurter Tor.** These are a result of the socialist building passion of the 1950s. It all contrasts rather sharply with **Simon-Dach-Strasse** a bit farther on. This street is famous for the Kneipenmeile, which features the most bars per square mile in all of Berlin. It goes without saying that it's always bustling with tourists.

Boxhagener Platz is a vibrant and fun place, especially on weekends, when there's a market in the square. The surrounding streets have many original clothing stores, galleries, and places to grab lunch.

The longest remaining piece of the Wall is the **East Side Gallery.** It's similar to an open-air museum and is on the must-see list for most visitors to Berlin. It's not authentic, though: The original painted part is on the West side, not the East. Nowadays this former no-man's-land alongside the Wall is occupied by up-and-coming media companies, as well as larger organizations like MTV, Universal, and the massive Mercedes-Benz Arena (a thorn in the side of the left-wing population).

SHORT ON TIME? HERE ARE THE HIGHLIGHTS
+ KARL-MARX-ALLEE + EAST SIDE GALLERY + URBAN SPREE
+ BOXHAGENER PLATZ + OBERBAUMBRÜCKE

TIPS
// This area is young, raw, and somewhat disorganized
// Great for a late-day walk because of the many bars and restaurants
// The first part is very bikeable

FRIEDRICHSHAIN

1. Kino International
2. Café Sibylle
3. Frankfurter Tor / Karl-Marx-Allee
4. Schoene Schreibwaren
5. Liebe Møbel Haben
6. Getränkefeinkost
7. Aufschnitt
8. Weder gestern noch morgen
9. Sometimes Coloured
10. Boxhagener Platz
11. Buchbox!
12. hhv.de Store / Lassrollen
13. Simon-Dach-Straße
14. Cupcake
15. Stereoki
16. Victoria met Albert
17. Visby
18. Schwesterherz / Küchenliebe
19. Hops & Barley
20. Schneeweiß
21. Datscha
22. Olivia
23. No hablo Español
24. RAW-tempel
25. Urban Spree
26. Veganz / Goodies
27. Oberbaum City
28. Michelberger Hotel
29. Oberbaumbrücke
30. East Side Gallery
31. East Side Park
32. YAAM

LEGEND

>> SIGHTS & ATTRACTIONS
>> FOOD & DRINK
>> SHOPPING
>> MORE TO EXPLORE

WALK 3 DESCRIPTION (approx. 3.1 miles)

If you don't mind a few extra miles and you love architecture, start at Kino International ❶; otherwise, go farther east and start at museum Café Sibylle ❷. The two towers belong to Frankfurter Tor, the gate to Karl-Marx-Allee ❸ . The street eventually becomes Frankfurter Allee. Follow this until you get to Nieder-barnimstrasse and take a right. This is a great place to shop ❹, or to have breakfast or a drink. Walk on until you get to Boxhagener Strasse. Turn right to find two awesome shops ❺ ❻. The route continues left, past a shop that sells stuffed toy "sausages" ❼. Go right onto Gärtnerstrasssse ❽. At Grünberger Strasse you can turn left for vintage goods ❾, otherwise turn right in the direction of Boxhagenerplatz ❿, which has a great market on the weekend. On the square is a book shop ⓫. If you love to skate, walk onward ⓬, otherwise take a left. Simon-Dach-Strasse ⓭ has the most bars in Berlin. You can stroll up and down this street, but the walk continues left to Krossener Strasse past Cupcake ⓮ and men's fashion ⓯. Diagonally across the street on the inter-section with Gärtnerstrasse you'll find Victoria met Albert ⓰. Turn right and walk through Gärtnerstrasse ⓱ ⓲ ⓳. The street makes a sharp right and becomes Simplonstrasse. Here you'll find the most entertaining restaurant of the neighbor-hood, Schneeweiss ⓴. Turn right onto Gabriel-Max-Strasse for Russian breakfast ㉑. Buy something tasty to go on Wühlischstrasse ㉒, or continue on and have a burrito ㉓. You'll leave the residential area through Libauer Strasse. Walk in the direction of the RAW-tempel ㉔ art center annex bar Urban Spree ㉕. Head through Revaler Strasse to Warschauer Strasse. On the other side on the left you'll find a vegan supermarket ㉖ where you can also have lunch. If you don't cross the street, cross the bridge to visit the Oberbaum City ㉗ behind the U-Bahn station. One of the most fun hotels in Berlin is Michelberger ㉘. Walk to the bridge and look at one of the prettiest bridges in town ㉙. Double back and visit the East Side Gallery ㉚ on Mühlenstrasse. Behind it is a park where you'll have a magnificent view of the sunset ㉛. If you're looking for more action, head to urban beach YAAM ㉜—tons of fun!

SIGHTS & ATTRACTIONS

① **Kino International** opened its doors two years after the Wall was built. It was the showpiece of the GDR. Restaurant Moskou on the other side is another interesting monument. This part of Karl-Marx-Allee is a must-see for anyone interested in architecture. Catch a movie in the evening and pop into Bar Babette for an after-show drink.

karl-marx-allee 33, www.kino-international.com, see website for times and prices, u-bahn u5 schillingstrasse

③ The two remarkable towers of **Frankfurter Tor** flank the impressive **Karl-Marx-Allee.** On both sides of the 1.4-mile-long boulevard are monumental building blocks that feel more like you're in Moscow than in Berlin. It's not surprising, considering these "workers' palaces" were built in the 1950s using the Soviet capital as an example. They're built in the so-called Zuckerbäcker style with ornamental decorations, columns, and sand-colored tiles.

karl-marx-allee, u-bahn u5 frankfurter tor

㉗ The old brick factory area of **Oberbaum City** used to be called "Lampen-stadt"—Lamp City. This is where Osram once produced its light bulbs. Now the renovated industrial buildings mostly house new-media companies and creative startups.

warschauer platz / rotherstrasse, s-bahn, u-bahn u1 warschauer strasse

㉙ Berlin has more bridges than Venice, and **Oberbaumbrücke** is by far the most beautiful. This bridge of red bricks was built at the end of the 19th century as a customs office for boats entering the city. During the Cold War it was used as border control between East (Friedrichshain) and West (Kreuzberg). The bridge is especially enchanting at night.

warschauer strasse/skalitzer strasse, s-bahn, u-bahn u1 warschauer strasse

㉚ This is where the river Spree used to divide East and West Berlin. On Mühlen-strasse, right at the water, you'll find the longest remaining section of the Berlin Wall—0.8 miles long. After the Wall fell, and following the German reunification in 1990, 118 artists from 21 countries decorated this section with artwork and

named it the **East Side Gallery.** The Gallery was renovated in 2009, 20 years after the fall of the Wall.

mühlenstrasse, www.eastsidegallery-berlin.de, s-bahn, u-bahn u1 warschauer strasse

FOOD & DRINK

⑧ Salads, soups, scrambled eggs: Everything at **Weder gestern noch morgen** is made with love. Choose from different types of breakfast: French, English, German, or even vegan.

gärtnerstrasse 22, fb wedergesternnochmorgen, t: 03089569615, open wed-fri 8:30am-6:30pm, sat-sun 8:30am-6pm, price €6, u-bahn u5 samariterstrasse

⑬ **Simon-Dach-Strasse** has more bars than anywhere else in Berlin. When the sun sets, people (mostly students and backpackers) flock to this street with low prices. You usually won't pay more than €4 for a cocktail. Rather have a beer in peace? Walk past the cocktail bars and go to Dachkammer at #39 (go upstairs for a real cozy feel) or Blechbilderbar at #35. And at Simonuno at #1 you won't find drinks, but rather cute little Berlin backpacks made of linen with nice prints.

simon-dach-strasse, s-bahn, u-bahn u1 warschauer strasse

⑭ **Cupcake** was the first shop in Berlin to actually sell cupcakes and they're still going strong. They create some exciting combinations, such as "The King," with banana and peanut butter, and "Pretty in Pink," a flashback to the '80s.

krossener strasse 12, www.cupcakeberlin.de, t: 03025768687, open mon-tue 1pm-9pm, wed-sun noon-7pm, price €3, s-bahn, u-bahn u1 warschauer strasse

⑲ If you want to taste an authentic beer from Friedrichshain, go to brewery **Hops & Barley.** They brew three types of beer: *Pilsner, Dunkel,* and *Weizen.* On Sunday evening the TV is switched on for the German crime series *Tatort.*

wühlischstrasse 22-23, www.hopsandbarley-berlin.de, t: 03029367534, open mon-fri 5pm-3am, sat-sun 3pm-3am, price €3.50, s-bahn, u-bahn u1 warschauer strasse, s-bahn ostkreuz

⑳ **Schneeweiss** attracts hipsters from all over town—and it's telling if someone from Mitte or Charlottenburg leaves their chic *Kiez* (neighborhood) to go to the more anarchist Friedrichshain. *The New York Times* tipped this bright restaurant with the words, "Forget Bratwurst, for lighter German fare go to Schneeweiss."
simplonstrasse 16, www.schneeweiss-berlin.de, t: 03029049704, open mon-fri noon-3pm & 6pm-11pm, sat-sun 10am-4pm & 6pm-11pm, price €20, s-bahn, u-bahn u1 warschauer strasse

㉑ Go to **Datscha** for traditional Russian food with a contemporary twist. Their *Kolchos*—farmers' breakfast—is delicious, and so are the *Blinis*. On Sundays they serve brunch. The place itself is very homey, with comfortable chairs and photographs on the walls.
gabriel-max-strasse 1, www.cafe-datscha.de, t: 03070086735, open mon-sat starting 10am, sun 9am-3pm, price €11, s-bahn, u-bahn u1 warschauer strasse

㉓ Funny enough, the owners of the tiny **No Hablo Español** do speak Spanish—and more. Their dishes are inspired by authentic Mexican cuisine, but influenced by flavors from all over the world. Order a burrito or quesadillas to go (the Indian burrito or chorizo and cheddar quesadilla are worth trying). Delish! Vegetarians and vegans will not be disappointed here, either.
kopernikusstrasse 22, t: 03095609351, open mon-sat noon-11pm, price €5, s-bahn, u-bahn u1 warschauer strasse

㉖ Berlin is well-known as a city that favors all things organic, despite all those Currywursts. **Veganz** is the largest vegan supermarket in Europe with more than 6,000 different products. From cookies to pizza and from sauces to superfoods, vegans will find whatever they need here. **Goodies** (in the supermarket) serves delicious vegan foods. With smoothies, wraps, and salads, it can be difficult to choose from their large menu. Can't eat another bite? Ask them to wrap your cake to go! Just above Veganz you'll find the very popular The Bowl that follows clean-eating practices. Their delicious meals are not only vegan, but their ingredients are also all-natural, organic, and unprocessed, for healthy enjoyment.
warschauer strasse 33, www.veganz.de, t: 03029009435, veganz open mon-sat 9am-10pm, goodies open mon-fri 7am-8pm, sat-sun 9am-8pm, s-bahn, u-bahn u1 warschauer strasse

㉘ The **Michelberger Hotel** has nice rooms, a great bar, and a lovely restaurant. They serve breakfast and dinner from Tuesday to Saturday. The menu is small but very good, with dishes made with local and seasonal products.

warschauer strasse 39-40, www.michelbergerhotel.com, t: 03029778590, breakfast mon-fri 7am-11am, sat-sun 8am-noon, lunch mon-fri noon-3pm, dinner tue-sat 7-11pm, price €16, s-bahn, u-bahn u1 warschauer strasse

SHOPPING

④ Displaying beautiful pens in leather cases, **Schoene Schreibwaren** is a paradise for anyone who loves to write with real ink. Next to the shop is a bookbinder that sells the notebooks and albums made in the shop. They have a second location on Weinbergsweg.

niederbarnimstrasse 6, www.schoeneschreibwaren.com, t: 017662893430, open mon-fri 10am-7pm, sat 10am-6pm, u-bahn u5 samariterstrasse, frankfurter tor

⑤ If you love unique furniture from the '50s and '60s, **Liebe Møbel Haben** is the place to go. It's filled with mostly Scandinavian and Italian design classics. In addition to tables and chairs, they also sell lamps and accessories that just might fit in your luggage.

boxhagener strasse 113, www.liebemoebelhaben.de, t: 03064490239, open tue-fri noon-6pm, sat 11-5pm, u-bahn u5 frankfurter tor

⑥ There is a huge number of *Spätis*—late-night shops selling liquor, candy, and cigarettes—in this city. It's almost easy to forget there are other liquor stores, too, such as **Getränkefeinkost.** Looking for that one special bottle? Make sure to pay this place a visit. They sell 350 types of beer, 100 types of lemonade, and much more.

boxhagener strasse 24, www.getraenkefeinkost.de, t: 03025933800, open mon-fri 1pm-8pm, sat 11am-8pm, u-bahn u5 frankfurter tor

⑦ **Aufschnitt** offers design and lifestyle products, textiles, and home accessories. It's a collaboration between several designers and they sell very unique products, including the designs of fashion label YV*L, by Yvonne Lamprecht.

There's an original butcher's case filled with cuddly toys, neck pillows, and hair-pins all in the shape of sausages.

boxhagener strasse 32, www.aufschnitt.net, t: 03063371548, open tue-fri noon-8pm, sat 2pm-6pm, u-bahn u5 samariterstrasse

⑨ Many vintage stores have racks and racks full of clothing, but not at **Sometimes Coloured.** This shop has a smart selection of clothing and accessories at varying prices. Their philosophy: There's enough clothing in the world, and one person's fashion mistake is another person's new look.

grünberger strasse 90, www.sometimescoloured.de, t: 03029352075, open tue-fri noon-8pm, sat 11am-7pm, u-bahn u5 samariterstrasse

⑪ **Buchbox!** is a so-called *Kiezbuchhandlung*—a neighborhood bookshop. They promote reading and organize events with authors who talk about their books. Bonus: The people that work here are enthusiastic and knowledgeable.

grünberger strasse 68, www.buchboxberlin.de, t: 03020078243, open mon-sat 9:30am-8:30pm, u-bahn u5 samariterstrasse, frankfurter tor

⑫ RAW-tempel has a skate park, and just around the corner you'll find two skateboard shops. Go to the **hhv.de Store** if you're looking for a more classic board, cool sneakers, and vinyl. This is the place to listen to records the old-fashioned way. At **Lassrollen** you'll find longboards and anything else a skate-boarder would need.

grünberger strasse 54 / grünberger strasse 42, www.hhv.de, www.lassrollen.de, t: 03029367377, hhv.de open mon-sat noon-8pm, lassrollen open mon 1pm-7pm, tue-fri 11am-8pm, sat 11am-6pm, u-bahn u5 frankfurter tor

⑮ From cool sneakers to trendy sunglasses—anything a man could wish for, **Stereoki** sells. This clothing store is geared toward men and they only sell hip items. Berlin wouldn't be the same without it.

gabriel-max-strasse 18, stereoki.com, t: 03053794667, open mon-fri 11:30am-8pm, sat 11am-7pm, s-bahn, u-bahn u1 warschauer strasse

⑯ **Victoria met Albert** is for "the woman who has everything and the man who doesn't need anything." You'll find nice clothing from different North European

brands, shoes, and accessories, but also colorful home accessories and gifts for kids. They have another location in Prenzlauer Berg.

krossenerstrasse 9-10, www.victoriametalbert.com, t: 03029774366, open mon-sat 11am-8pm, u-bahn u5 samariterstrasse, s-bahn ostkreuz

(17) **Visby** is a beautiful and light store that sells women's apparel from Scandinavian labels: Nümph, Modström, Rules by Mary, and mbyM. They also have stylish bags and shoes.

gärtnerstrasse 26, www.visby-berlin.de, t: 03081808418, open tue-fri noon-8pm, sat 11am-6pm, u-bahn u5 samariterstrasse, s-bahn ostkreuz

(18) **Schwesterherz** is a treasure trove of stunning paper products, cards, colorful crockery, and Berlin-style gifts. In the back of the store is a wall full of wrapping paper that's almost too pretty to use. There's also a juice bar that sells good smoothies. Next door is their shop **Küchenliebe,** with everything for the home chef: great pots and pans from Le Creuset, barista equipment, and professional knives. They also sell nice souvenirs for the kitchen and honey from Berlin.

gärtnerstrasse 28, www.schwesterherz-berlin.de, t: 03077901183, open mon-fri 11am-8pm, sat 10:30am-7pm, u-bahn u5 samariterstrasse, s-bahn ostkreuz

(22) **Olivia** is a paradise for everyone with a sweet tooth, full of Austrian chocolate bars, blackcurrant-truffle cakes and cookies of all sorts. Buy something to take home, or order a cup of coffee, take a seat on the cute little patio, and enjoy.

wühlischstrasse 30, www.olivia-berlin.de, t: 03060500368, open mon-sat noon-7pm, sun 1pm-6pm, s-bahn, u-bahn u1 warschauer strasse

MORE TO EXPLORE

(2) This location has been home to a *Kaffeehaus* ever since the 1950s, and thankfully **Café Sibylle** was spared during the redevelopment of the boulevard in the 1990s. Many of its original details are still intact. Their permanent exposition of the Karl-Marx-Allee and its "workers' palaces" is truly impressive.

karl-marx-allee 72, www.cafe-sibylle.de, t: 03029352203, open daily 10am-8pm, price pie €3, u-bahn u5 strausberger platz

⑩ On **Boxhagener Platz,** or *"Boxi,"* as it's lovingly called, there's always a group of old-timer Friedrichshainers hanging around with a beer in hand. The best farmers market in town is held on Saturdays, and it's the place to be on Sundays if you like flea markets and a good lunch. Both the square and the surrounding streets are full of places that offer unlimited brunch buffets. Our favorite brunch spot is just around the corner, at Silo (Gabriel-Max-Strasse #4). They don't have a buffet, but their brunch menu is incredible (try the poached eggs).

grünberger strasse, weekly market open sat 8am-2:30pm, flea market open sun 10am-6pm, u-bahn u5 samariterstrasse

㉔ **RAW-tempel,** located in the former Reichsbahn (German National Railway) rail yard, is a place where alternative culture thrives. The old warehouses behind the high gates are now home to clubs Cassiopeia (which has a great biergarten, also open during the day) and Suicide Circus, concert hall Astra, the Skatehalle *(www.skatehalle-berlin.de),* and a climbing wall. On Sundays there is a flea market and in the summer they organize open-air movie nights. The super-hip urban lounge bar Haubentaucher has an open-air pool between the walls of one of the warehouses.

revaler strasse 99, www.raw-tempel.de, t: 0302924695, open area is always accessible, opening times for venues vary, s-bahn, u-bahn u1 warschauer strasse

㉕ In the heart of Friedrichshain, on the grounds of RAW-tempel, is a huge space called **Urban Spree.** This modern space features fascinating street art. They have exhibitions, events, workshops, and sometimes even pop-up restaurants and fashion shows. There's a large bar where you can eat.

revaler strasse 99, www.urbanspree.com, open hours vary, s-bahn, u-bahn u1 warschauer strasse

㉛ The border between East and West is now home to **East Side Park.** Ever since the stadium was built, this part of the banks of the Spree has gotten a proper boost. At the start of the East Side Gallery is a souvenir shop where you can go through the Wall—it's quite the experience. Wander along the river and enjoy the sunset from Oberbaumbrücke.

mühlenstrasse, between east side gallery and spree, s-bahn, u-bahn u1 warschauer strasse

YOU
DRINK
COFFEE
I DRINK
TEA
MY DEAR.

P&T

㉜ *"Das* **YAAM** *ist wieder geöffnet"* ("The YAAM is open again") is music to the ears of everyone who loves this urban beach next to the Schillingbrücke. It's a city beach, sports complex, kids club, restaurant, and club all in one. A great place to visit at the end of a long day!

an der schillingbrücke, www.yaam.de, t: 0306151354, open hours vary depending on the weather, s-bahn ostbahnhof

WALK **4**

CHARLOTTENBURG & SCHÖNEBERG

ABOUT THE WALK

This walk is long and varied. The beautiful contrast between chic Charlottenburg and exciting Schöneberg makes for a nice introduction to the old West. There is a lot of culture and green space, but also great shopping and some classic restaurants and bars. Want to end with dinner? Then follow this walk in reverse.

THE NEIGHBORHOODS

In the 1970s and '80s Charlottenburg and Schöneberg (and also the nearby Wilmersdorf) were considered the heart of West Berlin. Tourists would arrive by train at the infamous **Bahnhof Zoo** to be welcomed by junkies, and they'd stay in one of the hotels on Kurfürstendamm. After the Wall fell, the focus shifted to the East part of the city, and West Berlin quickly began losing popularity. Famous theaters and traditional coffee houses closed their doors, and when **Hauptbahnhof** (Central Station) opened its doors in 2006, passenger trains began to rush straight past Bahnhof Zoo.

But as they say in Berlin: *"Totgesagte leben länger"* (literally "the condemned live longer," German for: "You can't keep a good man down"). The West overcame its image problems and is regaining its popularity. This is partly thanks to concept-mall **Bikini Berlin** and the relocation of the notorious **C/O Berlin** photography museum from Mitte to here. This neighborhood, filled with chic shops around **Kurfürstendamm** (or Ku'damm) and the famous department store KaDeWe, is the most cosmopolitan part of Berlin. Wide boulevards and little squares with French flair characterize the area.

Marlene Dietrich was born in Schöneberg, and the musical *Cabaret* originated here, as well. In the 1920s and '30s hedonism was rampant in Schöneberg, and David Bowie wrote a few of his most famous songs here in the 1970s.

Nowadays it's mostly known as the heart of gay Berlin, which is palpable in the shops and bars around **Nollendorfplatz.** Schöneberg is making a comeback—the area is very popular with young families, which is evident with the arrival of more luxury shops. South of Nollendorfplatz you'll find **Winterfeldtplatz,** home to the largest market in Berlin. And at Rathaus Schöneberg, J.F. Kennedy spoke his famous words, *"Ich bin ein Berliner."*

SHORT ON TIME? HERE ARE THE HIGHLIGHTS
+ KADEWE + GEDÄCHTNISKIRCHE + C/O BERLIN + SAVIGNYPLATZ + WINTERFELDTPLATZ

TIPS
// A classic, varied walk for first-time visitors to Berlin
// Suitable at the end of the day (shops close early on Saturdays)
// A good route to bike

CHARLOTTENBURG & SCHÖNEBERG

WALK 4 DESCRIPTION (approx. 5.1 miles)

Start with a visit to the Käthe-Kollwitz-museum ❶ or the Literaturhaus Berlin ❷. Walk to Kurfürstendamm, turn left, and cross the street. Head onto Grolmanstrasse. Halfway down this street is a concept store ❸. Go underneath the train tracks and stop for coffee ❹ on the beautiful Savignyplatz ❺ or browse some books ❻. Go left around the square, cross Kantstrasse, and take a left. A bit further on you can get Chinese food for dinner ❼, or follow the walk right onto Bleibtreustrasse ❽. At the end of the street, turn right and right again for coffee on Grolmanstrasse ❾. Walk back in the direction of Savignyplatz, go left around the square, and cross Kantstrasse again. Take a left ❿ ⓫ and another left onto Fasanenstrasse and a right when you get to Hardenbergstrasse. Here you'll find two beautiful photo museums ⓬ ⓭. If you go underneath the train tracks you'll end up at Zoo Berlin ⓮. Walk through Budapester Strasse past a mall ⓯. In the 25hours Hotel you can stop for a bite to eat or a drink on the 9th floor ⓰; the ground floor serves pizza ⓱. Cross Budapester Strasse towards Gedächtniskirche ⓲. Here you'll cross Ku'damm again and turn left to KaDeWe ⓳. Consider taking a detour via the Bauhaus-Archiv ⓴. Now you're leaving the Charlottenburg neighborhood. Walk a lengthy stretch on Ansbacher Strasse, past typical postwar apartment blocks, in the direction of Schöneberg. Turn left onto Geisbergstrasse and then right at Welserstrasse. Explore Viktoria-Luise-Platz ㉑ and take a left onto Winterfeldtstrasse. At Eisenacher Strasse go left and immediately right onto Nollendorfstrasse ㉒. Head to the right toward market square Winterfeldtplatz ㉓ when you reach Maassenstrasse, or make your way to an antique store ㉔. Walk down Goltzstrasse, where you can stop for a bite to eat ㉕ ㉖ or to shop ㉗. Cross Grunewaldstrasse. Across from the church is a great place to eat ㉘ and shop ㉙ ㉚. Walk back a bit and turn left onto Belziger Strasse ㉛. Take the first right and then immediately left for a bistro ㉜, or choose from the many restaurants in this neighborhood. Walk through Wartburgstrasse and turn left onto Gothaer Strasse. Take a right on Meininger Strasse. Cross busy Martin-Luther-Strasse to reach Rathaus Schöneberg ㉝ and the nearby Rudolph-Wilde-Park ㉞. And now, take a breather!

SIGHTS & ATTRACTIONS

① In the **Käthe-Kollwitz-Museum** you'll learn everything about one of the most famous female German artists: Käthe Kollwitz (1867-1945). She made sculptures, drawings, etchings, and lithographs. A socially engaged woman, she used her art to reveal the horrors of the two world wars.

fasanenstrasse 24, www.kaethe-kollwitz.de, t: 0308825210, open daily 11am-6pm, entrance €6, u-bahn u1 uhlandstrasse

⑤ **Savignyplatz** was built at the start of the 19th century and withstood the popularity of the East once the Wall had fallen. The square is still very elegant with many restaurants, galleries, a bookstore underneath the arcades of the S-Bahn, and a stunning shoe shop.

savignyplatz, s-bahn savignyplatz

⑫ Photography museum **C/O Berlin** used to be located in the post office in Mitte, but it has found a new home in the Amerika Haus. Visit the website for information on current expositions.

hardenbergstrasse 22-24, www.co-berlin.org, t: 03028444160, open daily 11am-8pm, entrance €10, s-bahn u-bahn u2, u9 zoologischer garten

⑬ Helmut Newton was born in 1920 in Berlin as Helmut Neustädter. The **Helmut Newton Foundation** was founded after the famous photographer's death in 2004. It's an impressive building with different exhibitions of Newton's works, as well as those of his wife, photographer Alice Springs.

jebensstrasse 2, www.helmutnewton.com, t: 03031864856, open tue-wed & fri 10am-6pm, thu 10am-8pm, sat-sun 11am-6pm, entrance €10, s-bahn u-bahn u2, u9 zoologischer garten

⑱ Nowhere else can you witness the devastating effects of the bombings during World War II as at the **Gedächtniskirche**. The damaged old church, together with a new rectangular church hall, is one of the most important monuments in the city. Extensive renovations have been underway since 2010.

breitscheidplatz, www.gedaechtniskirche-berlin.de, t: 0302185023, open daily 9am-7pm, free entrance and tour, u-bahn u1, u9 kurfürstendamm

Helmut Newton | Alice Spr

㉑ If you love architecture, you must visit **Bauhaus-Archiv.** Bauhaus operated from 1919 to 1933, when it was forced to close during the Nazi regime. It was a progressive school for artists and architects that focused on function and minimalism. The school started in Dessau but spent its final year in Berlin. Various famous teachers have left their mark on the Bauhaus, such as Mies van der Rohe, Gropius, Klee, and Kandinsky. The museum shows all aspects of the movement: Architecture, furniture, photography, stage, and theater.

klingelhöferstrasse 14, www.bauhaus.de, t: 0302540020, open wed-mon 10am-5pm, entrance €7 wed-fri, €8 sat-mon, u-bahn u1, u2, u3, u4 nollendorfplatz

㉑ Many streets in Schöneberg end at **Viktoria-Luise-Platz**—a hexagonal square with a large fountain in the middle. It's named after the daughter of Emperor Wilhelm II. The cafés and restaurants are very popular with the locals. Film director Billy Wilder lived here in the 1920s at #11.

viktoria-luise-platz, u-bahn u4 viktoria-luise-platz

FOOD & DRINK

④ Savignyplatz has a distinct French vibe, especially in the summer. Restaurant **Brel,** named for the famous Belgian singer Jacques Brel, feels very Parisian with its patio chairs and tables with crisp white linen. The menu showcases classic dishes like *moules-frites* (mussels and fries) and blood sausage. The owner also has a bar just around the corner, on Jeanne-Mammen-Bogen 576-577, called **Gainsbourg**—aptly named after the famous French crooner Serge Gainsbourg.

Savignyplatz 1, www.cafebrel.de, t: 03031800020, open daily 9am-1am, s-bahn savignyplatz

⑦ A Chinese restaurant called **Good Friends** doesn't inspire a lot of confidence, but don't worry—this is the place to be for amazing and authentic Cantonese food. The menu is partly in Chinese and many of the patrons are Chinese as well, which is always a good sign. The restaurant is famous for its duck.

kantstrasse 30, www.goodfriends-berlin.de, t: 0303132659, open daily noon-1am, s-bahn savignyplatz

⑨ **Café Savigny** has that authentic *Kaffeehauskultur* (coffee-house culture). Sit down with coffee, a small glass of water, and a newspaper, and you're set for hours. The café has a large selection of international magazines as well. You can order breakfast until late in the afternoon, and in the summer they have outdoor seating. Explore the surrounding streets—there's plenty to discover.
grolmanstrasse 53-54, facebook cafesavigny, t: 017614435046, open daily 9am-midnight, s-bahn savignyplatz

⑩ The **Schwarzes Café** is popular with tourists and Berliners alike because it's one of the few places in Charlottenburg that offers a hot meal 24 hours a day. We recommend the *Frühstück Späte Liebe* or Love on the Run after a long night out on the town.
kantstrasse 148, www.schwarzescafe-berlin.de, t: 0303138038, open wed-mon 24hrs, tue closed 3am-10am, price €8, s-bahn savignyplatz

⑪ **Paris Bar** is one of the most famous restaurants in Germany. Its notoriety comes not from the food, which is French, but from its celebrity status. Madonna, Robert de Niro, Gorbachev, and Yves Saint-Laurent have all eaten in this restaurant, surrounded by unusual artwork. The interior was designed by artist Martin Kippenberger. In 2009 his painting *Paris Bar* was auctioned off for $2.5 million.
kantstrasse 152, www.parisbar.de, t: 0303138052, open daily noon-2am, price €28, u-bahn u1 uhlandstrasse

⑯ On the top floor of the 25hours Hotel, part of the Bikini Berlin complex, is restaurant **Neni Berlin.** They serve a unique mix of small Russian, Spanish, German, and Arabic bites meant to share. The view of the Zoo is stunning and in the summertime you can eat outside. Next door is **Monkey Bar**—the hottest new spot in the old West.
budapester strasse 40, www.25hours-hotels.com, t: 030120221200, open neni mon-fri noon-11pm, sat-sun 12:30pm-11pm, monkey bar open sun-thu noon-1am, fri-sat noon-2am, price €17, s-bahn, u-bahn u2, u9 zoologischer garten

⑰ In the mood for a good pizza? Head to **L'Osteria.** It's a well-known chain in Germany, but this particular branch is very beautifully decorated. They serve

gigantic pizzas and very good pastas in a busy and bustling environment. And don't skip dessert!

budapester strasse 40, www.losteria.de, t: 03025794325, open mon-sat 11am-midnight, sun noon-midnight, price €10, s-bahn, u-bahn u2, u9 zoologischer garten

㉒ **Stagger Lee** was a murderer who became a legend, inspiring many a song-writer like Bob Dylan and Nick Cave. It's also the name of one of the most fun bars in Schöneberg, with its western-saloon vibe. Order a Mint Julep, or their signature "Robert Mitchum": A shot of Tequila that comes with a box of matches and a *Lucky Strike*. Park yourself in a leather loveseat, or walk through the saloon doors for a smoke. You'll feel like you've landed in an old-fashioned Western movie.

nollendorfstrasse 27, www.staggerlee.de, t: 03029036158, open daily 7pm-2am, price €9, u-bahn u1, u2, u3, u4 nollendorfplatz

㉕ In 2007 coffee house **Sorgenfrei** opened its doors. Its philosophy is rooted in the nostalgic idea that everything was better in the old days. The owners love the 1950s and '60s, and it shows in this former butchery. Even the menu is retro, with dishes like *toast Hawaii* (grilled cheese with ham and pineapple), profiter-oles, and other deliciousness "the way momma used to make it". Most of the furniture, plate settings, and vintage accessories are for sale.

goltzstrasse 18, www.sorgenfrei-in-berlin.de, t: 03030104071, open tue-fri noon-7pm, sat 10am-6pm, sun 1pm-6pm, price €6, u-bahn u1, u2, u3, u4 nollendorfplatz

㉖ Berlin is home to countless small Turkish restaurants, but only a few are worth trying. **Meyan-Süssholz** (meaning "licorice root") is one of the great ones. Their cabinets are filled with delicacies and crockery, and the center of the shop has a large showcase for all their food. Choose a few dishes that look most tempting to you (a difficult task with the large selection). On the weekend they serve breakfast, which is a real crowd pleaser!

goltzstrasse 36, www.meyan-berlin.de, t: 03075442540, open mon-fri 10am-11pm, sat 9am-11pm, sun 10am-6pm, price mezze €5, u-bahn u1, u2, u3, u4 nollendorfplatz

㉘ No matter how busy it gets, the vibe is always very relaxed in **Gasthaus Gottlob.** While one person is reading a paper and enjoying a coffee with milk, someone else is in the middle of writing a short story. Munch on a typical *Süss-kartoffelstrudel* (sweet potato tart) or *Käsespätzle* (egg noodles with cheese) while sitting outside with a view of the Apostel Paulus Kirche.

akazienstrasse 17, t: 03078708095, open mon-thu 9am-1am, fri-sat 9am-2am, sun 10am-1am, u-bahn u7 eisenacher strasse

㉜ Restaurant Storch used to be a well-known name in the Berlin art-scene of the 1990s, but eventually had to close its doors. It was restored to part of its former glory in 2007 and was given a new name: **Renger-Patzsch.** The restaurant is named after a nature photographer whose work is exhibited inside. Come here for simple German food in a classic and cozy atmosphere. They are famous for their *Elsässer Flammkuchen* (Alsatian tarte flambée).

wartburgstrasse 54, www.renger-patzsch.com, open daily 6pm-11:30pm, price €17, flammkuchen €9, u-bahn u7 eisenacher strasse

SHOPPING

③ **Van Nord** is best described as a mini department or concept store. The shop is a great place to go for unique clothing, jewelry, and home accessories. Owner Andrea Ennen sources her products mostly in Northern Europe but some items, like perfume or pillows, come from places such as England and the US. Everything is beautiful.

grolmanstrasse 30-31, www.vannord.com, t: 03088768972, open mon-fri 11am-7pm, sat 11am-6pm, u-bahn u1 uhlandstrasse

⑥ The S-Bahn goes straight over the top of **Bücherbogen.** Take your time and browse through the large collection of art and cultural books in this shop. You'll find books about architecture, photography, graphic design, film, dance, and fashion.

savignyplatz, stadtbahnbogen 593, www.buecherbogen.com, t: 03031869511, open mon-fri 10am-8pm, sat 10am-7pm, s-bahn savignyplatz

⑧ **P & T Paper and Tea** sells different kinds of tea from around the world. Looking for a special blend, or an unusual green, white, yellow, or black tea?

This is where you'll find it. Just making a cup is an event here, and they'll teach you the fine art of tea making during a two-hour course. The shop also sells pretty cards and notebooks.

bleibtreustrasse 4, www.paperandtea.com, t: 03095615468, open mon-sat 11am-8pm, s-bahn savignyplatz

⑮ **Bikini Berlin** is a large mall with shops, flagship stores, and pop-up stores with fashion, electronics, art, and lifestyle brands from around the globe. Take a look, if only for the remarkable architecture of the building itself.

budapester strasse 38-50, www.bikiniberlin.de, t: 030120221200, shop and pop-up boxes open mon-sat 10am-8pm, mall mon-sat 9am-9pm, s-bahn u-bahn u2, u9 zoologischer garten

⑲ **KaDeWe** stands for Kaufhaus des Westens—the department store of the West. While the Berlin Wall was still standing, this department store, the largest in Europe, was the symbol of capitalism. It has six floors and sells anything your heart desires. You can eat on the top floor underneath a glass ceiling; the delicatessen department sells specialty foods from all over the world.

tauentzienstrasse 21-24, www.kadewe.de, t: 03021210, open mon-thu 10am-8pm, fri 10am-9pm, sat 9:30am-8pm, u-bahn u1, u2, u3 wittenbergplatz

㉔ **Antiquariat Mertens & Pomplun** sells old books and special editions, but you'll also find posters, vintage toys, maps, globes, and framed butterflies. The beautiful old pictures of Berlin are especially worth a look.

winterfeldtstrasse 51, www.mp-rarebooks.de, t: 0302519203, open mon-fri 11am-6:30pm, sat 10am-2pm, u-bahn u1, u2, u3, u4 nollendorfplatz

㉗ Your house should feel like a home. Some like it to be light and bright, but for those who love color, **Mobilien** is the place to be. It's filled with small furniture and colorful accessories for every room in your house.

goltzstrasse 13b, www.mobilien.de, t: 03071538675, open mon-fri 11am-7pm, sat 11am-5pm, u-bahn u7 kleistpark or eisenacher strasse

㉙ Design and quality are the main focus when proprietors **Greta & Luis** source their newest fashion collections. Sometimes they go for big names, and sometimes they choose new designers. They have a few locations—one in Mitte, one in Prenzlauer Berg, and another a bit farther along Akazienstrasse.

akazienstrasse 7a, www.gretaundluis.com, open mon-fri 11am-7pm, sat 10am-6pm, u-bahn u7 eisenacher strasse

(30) In the heart of Akazienkiez is the very first *Kochhaus* (cookhouse)—a rapidly-growing mini chain store. **Kochhaus Schöneberg** is a deluxe supermarket. They sell recipes with all the ingredients included. From fish and meat to starters and desserts—with nearly 20 recipes at a time, there is always plenty to choose from. The cabinets are filled with cookbooks, wine, tea, coffee, and herbs.

akazienstrasse 1, www.kochhaus.de, t: 030577089, open mon-sat 10am-9pm, u-bahn u7 eisenacher strasse, s-bahn julius-leber-brücke

(31) Schöneberg is a child-friendly neighborhood, and it shows when you enter **Friedland & Partner.** They sell clothing and accessories from Scandinavian brands like Bellerose and Bensimon for kids and moms.

belziger strasse 28, www.friedlandundpartner.de, t: 03078719502, open mon-fri 11am-7pm, sat 11am-4pm, u-bahn u7 eisenacher strasse

MORE TO EXPLORE

(2) **Literaturhaus Berlin** hosts literary exhibitions and events. Every Monday at 9pm you can attend a reading in Café Wintergarten while you enjoy light and tasty dishes. Bookshop Kohlhaas & Company is located in the same building.

fasanenstrasse 23, www.literaturhaus-berlin.de, t: 0308872860, see website for times and prices, café open daily 9am-midnight, u-bahn u1 uhlandstrasse

(14) The most famous inhabitant of the Zoologischer Garten (or **Zoo Berlin**) was ice bear Knut, who died in 2011. Thankfully the oldest zoo in Germany has many other popular occupants. Hippo Knautschke was the only zoo animal to survive World War II, and his descendants are still very much loved by the people of Berlin.

hardenbergplatz 8, www.zoo-berlin.de, t: 030254010, open daily summer 9am-6:30pm, winter 9am-5pm, entrance €14.50, s-bahn, u-bahn u2, u9 zoologischer garten

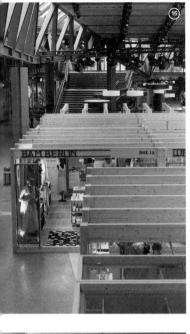

㉓ Every Wednesday and Saturday **Winterfeldtplatz** hosts the largest market in Berlin. It's a great place to stroll and browse. Delight in artisan breads and Turkish dips. Around the square you'll find many cafés, antique shops, and small boutiques.
Winterfeldtplatz, www.winterfeldt-markt.de, open wed 8am-2pm, sat 8am-4pm, u-bahn u1, u2, u3, u4 nollendorfplatz

㉝ Schöneberg used to be a city in its own right, hence why **Rathaus Schöneberg** (city hall) is so big. It was built between 1911 and 1914, and the West Berlin parliament was housed here until 1990. On June 26, 1963 Kennedy gave his famous *"Ich bin ein Berliner"* speech here. On the weekend they have a *Flohmarkt* (flea market). Go early to find something special.
john-f-kennedy-platz 1, flea market open sat-sun 9am-4pm, u-bahn u4 rathaus schöneberg

㉞ One of the most unique U-Bahn stations is in **Rudolph-Wilde-Park,** which used to be a lake. The station is on ground level. The U-Bahn dives back underground outside the park, but here the track runs above ground over a stone wall with high windows. The park has a large duck pond and is a favorite destination for runners and pedestrians alike. Be sure to check out Hirschbrunnen—a fountain with a golden stag and sculptures by Richard Guhr, a famous German sculptor. Or partake in a nice game of *boules* (bocce). All in all, this park is a great place to relax after a long day in the city!
martin-luther-strasse/fritz-elsas-strasse, u-bahn u4 rathaus schöneberg

WALK 5

KREUZBERG

ABOUT THE WALK

This walk is quite long, but very interesting. Note that the museums at the start are quite far from the U-Bahn station where the walk actually starts. As you wander through both parts of Kreuzberg, you'll get a good sense of modern-day Berlin, the city's need to build, and some very exciting projects. If you want to go out later on, you can extend this walk in the direction of Schlesischer Busch.

THE NEIGHBORHOODS

Kreuzberg is actually divided into two parts named after their old zip codes. **Kreuzberg 36** is also called SO 36—SO is *Südost* (southeast) and 36 refers to the zip code. During the years of the Wall this area was closed in on three sides, which resulted in the evolution of an alternative culture. Squatters, punks, artists, people on welfare, and Turkish immigrants lived peacefully side by side, united by their common hatred of the police during the annual Labor Day celebrations.

While squatters are less of a presence today and many of the other alternative inhabitants left for Wedding, Friedrichshain, and Moabit, the Turkish population remained—the largest community outside of Turkey. The neighborhood around **Oranienstrasse** is the center of Turkish Berlin, with restaurants, shops, and a Turkish bath house.

Kreuzberg 61, the other half of the neighborhood, is a bit more cosmopolitan and chic than SO 36, but it also has a very artistic feel about it. The neighborhood got its name from the hill in the beautiful Viktoriapark (*"Berg"*), named after the monumental cross (*"Kreuz"*) that commemorates the victory over Napoleon.

In recent years the **Graefekiez** has become a very popular residential area, which means there are more and more great places to eat and shop. This neighborhood borders Kreuzkölln—the northern part of Neukölln. Particularly beautiful are the streets around **Chamissoplatz,** with many old houses that survived World War II. These are a beloved backdrop for movies and television series.

On the other side of Mehringdamm is the large **Park am Gleisdreieck,** a former rail yard. The people from the neighborhood fought for this park, as it was once zoned for building. It's now a stunning green space where you can skate, run, or simply go for a walk.

SHORT ON TIME? HERE ARE THE HIGHLIGHTS
**+ BERLINISCHE GALERIE + MARKTHALLE NEUN + CHAMISSOPLATZ
+ LANDWEHRKANAL + PARK AM GLEISDREIECK**

TIPS

// Must-see after visiting Mitte and Charlottenburg
// Good for an evening walk and easy to follow in reverse direction
// Not the best route for cycling

KREUZBERG

WALK 5 DESCRIPTION (approx. 6.1 miles)

Start at the Jüdisches Museum ❶ or the Berlinische Galerie ❷, or go directly to Moritzplatz via U-Bahn. From here you can go to the Prinzessinnengarten ❸ or Planet Modulor ❹. Head down Oranienstrasse ❺ ❻ ❼ and visit Museum der Dinge ❽ or NGBK gallery ❾. Next door is concept store Voo ❿. Try to get a table at Bateau Ivre ⓫, and once you've eaten, turn left onto Mariannenstrasse. Walk straight on until you reach the statue of the firefighters, go around it to the right, and continue until you get to Mariannenplatz. In the park is a beautiful Kunstraum (art space) ⓬ with a restaurant. A bit further on is the remarkable Baumhaus ⓭. Just before that, take a right onto Wrangelstrasse. On the corner of Pücklerstrasse is restaurant Long March Canteen ⓮. Other food options are available in the Markthalle ⓯ ⓰. A bit farther down Pücklerstrasse is a great thrift store ⓱. Walk straight on, turn right at Waldemarstrasse and immediately left onto Manteuffelstrasse. Just before the train tracks, take a right onto Oranienstrasse and make a left at the square onto Mariannenstrasse. Go underneath the train tracks. Keep walking until you reach the Landwehrkanal ⓲. Take a little detour, or go straight over the bridge onto Graefestrasse ⓳. Turn right onto Dieffenbachstrasse ⓴ ㉑ ㉒. Go left on Grimmstrasse alongside the park, and then cross Urbanstrasse. Take a left before the Fichte-Bunker ㉓, or go right immediately onto Körtestrasse for some great places to explore ㉔. Follow the road towards the crossing with Hasenheide/Südstern. Cross and take a right on Bergmannstrasse. Walk across the cemetery ㉕ and, just before the graves, continue on the path onto Bergmannstrasse. This street offers tasty Austrian food ㉖ and plenty of shopping ㉗. Afterward, turn left on Friesenstrasse ㉘. Take the second right to reach Chamissoplatz ㉙ to get an idea of what Berlin once looked like. Walk around the square via Arndtstrasse and turn right on Nostitzstrasse. Take a left on Bergmannstrasse and a right at the pharmacy to reach Mehringdamm. Cross at the intersection of Gneisenaustrasse and Yorckstrasse and go left onto Mehringdamm. Time for a Currywurst ㉚ or kebab ㉛! Walk through Yorckstrasse and straight down Hornstrasse to Park am Gleisdreieck ㉜. Still not tired? Follow the signs for the Deutsches Technikmuseum ㉝ next to U-Bahn Gleisdreieck.

SIGHTS & ATTRACTIONS

① Be prepared—the **Jüdisches Museum** will leave you speechless, because what you see and read here is almost unimaginable. It's housed in an impressive building designed by Daniel Libeskind and you'll learn everything about the history of Jews in Germany from the Middle Ages to now.
lindenstrasse 9-14, www.jmberlin.de, t: 03025993300, open mon 10am-8pm, tue-sun 10am-8pm, entrance €8, u-bahn u1, u6 hallesches tor, u6 kochstrasse, u8 moritzplatz

② The **Berlinische Galerie** Museum of Modern Art houses a collection of Berlin art from 1870 to now. They have famous works from art movements that originated in Berlin, such as Dada, New Objectivity, and East European avant-garde. The pavement on the outside is decorated with bright yellow squares with black letters.
alte jakobstrasse 124-128, www.berlinischegalerie.de, t: 03078902600, open wed-mon 10am-6pm, entrance €8, u-bahn u6 kochstrasse, u8 moritzplatz

⑧ In the **Museum der Dinge**—the museum of things—you'll see various objects mostly from the 20th and 21st centuries. Any object that could have some historic design significance ends up in this museum. There's an open area where visitors can view all the items, along with temporary exhibitions. The website allows you to adopt things for a certain price. It's a serious practice, but executed with a playful wink.
oranienstrasse 25, www.museumderdinge.de, t: 03092106311, open mon & wed-sun noon-7pm, entrance €6, u-bahn u1, u8 kottbusser tor

⑨ From the street, the **NGBK** (Neue Gesellschaft für Bildende Kunst) looks like an ordinary bookstore, but behind it lies a large gallery. This is where the members of the NGBK decide on their exhibitions through a very democratic process. The works often have a socialist theme.
oranienstrasse 25, www.ngbk.de, t: 0306165130, open sun-wed noon-7pm, thu-sat noon-8pm, free entrance, u-bahn u1, u8 kottbusser tor

⑫ **Kunstraum Kreuzberg/Bethanien** dates back to the anarchistic 1970s, when this former hospital was occupied by squatters trying to rescue it from

demolition. The Neo-Gothic building has been a space for art exhibitions ever since. Restaurant 3Schwestern is a nice place to eat nearby.

mariannenplatz 2, www.kunstraumkreuzberg.de, t: 030902981455, open daily noon-7pm, free entrance, u-bahn u1 görlitzer bahnhof, u1, u8 kottbusser tor

⑬ The Wall created many abandoned areas in Berlin, but none of them are more outlandish than the **Baumhaus an der Mauer** (Treehouse at the Wall). In the 1980s Osman Kalin grew vegetables on a 3,700-square-foot fallow piece of land. Although officially part of East Berlin, it was located on the western side of the Wall and eventually fell into disuse. Kalin got permission to build a wooden house and after the Wall fell, he expanded his garden with a second house. Now Kalin's son manages the complex. The Baumhouse has no indoor access for visitors.

bethaniendamm/mariannenplatz, s-bahn ostbahnhof

㉕ The **cemeteries on Bergmannstrasse** consist of four different connected areas. It's a beautiful place to sit and enjoy the sunshine. The ornamental head-stones recall the wealth of old Berlin, although the city is now known as one of the poorest in the whole of Germany.

bergmannstrasse, open daily from 8am to 4pm-8pm (depending on the season), u-bahn u7 südstern

㉙ **Chamissoplatz** is located in one of the most beautiful neighborhoods of Berlin. Both the square and its surrounding streets are like an open-air museum; this is what the residential areas from before World War II looked like. The neighborhood wasn't bombed because the Allies wanted to spare the nearby Tempelhof airport. Don't be surprised if you find yourself in the middle of a film shoot—Chamissoplatz is a popular location for filmmakers to capture historic Berlin.

chamissoplatz, u-bahn u6 platz der luftbrücke

㉝ Trains, plains, automobiles, and boats: Anything remotely related to the history of technology is on display at the **Deutsches Technikmuseum.** They have exhibits on photography, as well as water- and windmills, and even a brewery.

trebbiner strasse 9, www.sdtb.de, t: 039902540, open tue-fri 9am-5:30pm, sat-sun 10am-6pm, entrance €8, u-bahn u1, u2 gleisdreieck

FOOD & DRINK

⑤ Mexican restaurant **Santa Maria** is located on busy Oranienstrasse, but you should be able to find a table at lunch time. Try the *taco campechanos* (tacos with different types of meat) or the *tostadas de hongos* (tortillas with mushrooms). At night the place is transformed into a bar with delicious cocktails and good food.

oranienstrasse 170, www.santaberlin.com, t: 03092210027, open daily starting at noon, price €6.50, u-bahn u1, u8 kottbusser tor

⑪ **Bateau Ivre** is located in a corner building with a sidewalk café on each side, and when the sun is out, they are both jam-packed. It's no wonder: The vibe is great, the food is good, and the service is quick—even on busy days! Try the full breakfast in the morning or a *Pastis* in the afternoon. In the evening they serve tapas, but you can also come in for just a beer (or two).

oranienstrasse 18, t: 03061403659, open sun-thu 9am-2am, fri-sat 9am-3am, price €8, u-bahn u8 kottbusser tor, u1 görlitzer bahnhof

⑭ "Let your chopsticks do the talking," is the motto at **Long March Canteen.** Octopus salad, thousand-year eggs, lotus leaves filled with rice, and shrimp: This is the place for one-of-a-kind Chinese dishes. Don't be fooled by its somewhat bleak and unobtrusive exterior—the interior is stunning: Simple and dark, with neon lights on the walls and a kitchen in the middle. It's one of the coolest restaurants in Berlin.

wrangelstrasse 20, www.longmarchcanteen.com, t: 01788849599, open daily 6pm-midnight, price small dishes €7, u-bahn u1 schlesisches tor, görlitzer bahnhof

⑮ **Weltrestaurant Markthalle** is a no-nonsense eaterie, but very loved by the people in the neighborhood. The main attraction is the gigantic schnitzels. This meat dish gained literary fame in the book *Herr Lehmann* by Sven Regeners. It tells about the ruin of Kreuzberg as the anarchistic paradise of West Berlin. The book has been turned into a movie, which was filmed mostly in the Markthalle.

pücklerstrasse 34, www.weltrestaurant-markthalle.de, t: 0306175502, open mon-fri from noon, sat-sun from 10am, price €14, u-bahn u1 görlitzer bahnhof

⑯ The large and monumental **Markthalle Neun,** built in 1891, was reopened as an indoor market hall a few years ago. On Friday and Saturday they sell artisan products: cakes, salads, cheeses, tapas, fruit, quiches, pies, pasta, organic tea— you name it. Order at one of the stalls and sit down at one of the small tables. The weekly Street Food Thursday features international bites and live music.

pücklerstrasse 34, www.markthalle9.de, market open fri noon-8pm, sat 10am-6pm, street food thursday thu 5pm-10pm, price snack €3-9, u-bahn u1 görlitzer bahnhof

⑲ At the intersection of Graefestrasse and Böckhstrasse you'll find many great little cafés on a square. One of the best, **Kaffeebar,** is an awesome place with an industrial look. They serve good coffee, tasty sandwiches, great cakes, and many more goodies. It's the perfect place for a good brunch, with many vegan and gluten-free options. When the weather is nice, try to secure a spot outside.

gräfestrasse 8, www.kaffeebar-berlin.com, open mon-fri 8am-7pm, sat-sun 9:30am-7pm, price €10, u-bahn u8 schönleinstrasse

㉑ The "boss" of Canadian pizzeria **Ron Telesky** is the large elk hanging on the wall, guarding all the gigantic pizzas sold whole and by the slice. Try the one with sweet potato and rosemary, or tandoori tofu, mango, and peanuts. A few drops of maple-chili syrup and you're in pizza heaven.

dieffenbachstrasse 62, t: 03061621111, open mon-fri 12:30pm-10pm, sat-sun 1:30pm-10pm, price whole pizza €20, slice €3, u-bahn u8 schönleinstrasse, u7 südstern

㉖ *Marillentopfenknödel* (apricot dumplings), *Würstel-Teller mit Kraut* (sausage with cabbage), and *Tafelspitz mit Apfelkren* (beefsteak with apple horseradish): At **Felix Austria** you can tuck into typical Austrian specialities and, of course, the menu showcases the *Wiener Schnitzel*. The restaurant has two separate entrances; the one on the left is used the most. The decor is simple, the food is good, and you can sit outside, weather permitting.

bergmannstrasse 26, www.felixaustria.de, t: 03061675451, open mon-sat 9am-midnight, sun 10am-midnight, price €12.50, u-bahn u7 gneisenaustrasse

㉚ If you're in need of a hearty breakfast after a late night out, go to **Curry 36** for the ultimate Berlin hangover cure. This is one of the most popular *Currywurst* stands in Berlin. On the weekend you may have to wait in line for about ten minutes, but to the real fans it's worth it.

mehringdamm 36, www.curry36.de, t: 0302517368, open daily 9am-5am, price €1.50, u-bahn u6, u7 mehringdamm

③ There's always a line at **Mustafa's Gemüse Kebap**—sometimes it takes about 15 minutes, sometimes more than an hour, but the vegetarian sandwich with roasted and raw veggies and feta cheese is worth the wait. They also sell meat varieties.

mehringdamm 32, www.mustafas.de, open daily 10am-2am, price €3, u-bahn u6, u7 mehringdamm

SHOPPING

⑥ Bakery **Melek Pastanesi** sells both German and Turkish breads and pastries. Baklava lies side by side with *Berliner Apfelkuchen* (Berlin-style apple pie), and they also sell pita breads and *Kaiserbrötchen* (German bread rolls). This is multicultural living at its best.

oranienstrasse 28, t: 0306145186, open daily 24 hours, u-bahn u1, u8 kottbusser tor

⑦ Feeling peckish after a night on the town? A healthier option for fries and *döner kebab* is served up at **Smyrna Kuruyemis:** dried fruits, nuts, and seeds from the Mediterranean. They roast the nuts in the back of the store, and the display cases are filled with figs, sugary almonds, and dates. Try the *sehzade sucuk,* a sausage made with walnuts and raisins.

oranienstrasse 27, t: 03061107181, open mon-fri 9am-2am, sat 10am-2am, u-bahn u1, u8 kottbusser tor

⑩ **VooStore** is hidden away in a courtyard. It's a huge space with a purposefully unfinished look and a beautiful collection of fashion, stationery, magazines, cosmetics, and gifts. The fashion is mostly from Scandinavian designers like Henrik Vibskov, Acne, and Wood Wood. There's also a coffee bar.

oranienstrasse 24, www.vooberlin.com, t: 0306957972710, open mon-sat 11am-8pm, u-bahn u1, u8 kottbusser tor

⑰ **Pony Hütchen,** named after a character in the German children's book *Emil and the Detectives,* is full of fun and colorful vintage items. They sell furniture, clothing, retro lamps, and more. Owner Lilli Nielsen sources her collection from all over Germany.

pücklerstrasse 33, www.pretty-stuff.de, t: 03069818679, open mon-fri 1pm-8pm, sat 11am-8pm, u-bahn u1 görlitzer bahnhof

⑳ Dieffenbachstrasse is a quickly up-and-coming street. One of the more recent additions is **Homage,** a store that sells responsibly-sourced fashion and accessories. Their keywords are upcycling, recycling, and social projects. Two noteworthy brands you'll find here are Simón Ese (clothing designed in Munich and made in Mexico) and Pastperfekt (secondhand items turned into beautiful lamps and furniture). They also sell bags made from recycled leather. The items are not just responsible, but also beautiful and trendy.

dieffenbachstrasse 15, www.homagestore.com, t: 03065007890, open tue-sat 11am-6pm, u-bahn u8 schönleinstrasse, u7 südstern

㉒ It's difficult to resist the urge to buy everything in **Süper Store.** Founded by a German designer and a Swiss artist, the shop offers stunning leather bags and wallets, jewelry, porcelain from the Czech Republic, and unique woolen blankets. Their assortment is small but spot-on.

dieffenbachstrasse 12, www.sueper-store.de, t: 03098327944, open tue-fri 11am-7pm, sat 11am-4pm, u-bahn u8 schönleinstrasse, u7 südstern

㉔ **Lindt,** housed in a former chocolate shop of the same name, is filled with clothing and accessories from years past. They sell mostly dresses from the 1960s, 1970s, and 1980s, but also newer items and unique accessories. Think vintage embroidered bags, a belt with a lion's head, pumps with houndstooth print, and other hidden gems. Their prices are reasonable, and they have a selection of menswear as well.

körtestrasse 16, www.lindt-second-hand-berlin.de, t: 0306917910, open mon-fri 3pm-7pm, sat by appointment only, u-bahn u7 südstern

㉗ The covered **Marheineke Markthalle** has been home to a market since as early as 1892. Nowadays they sell mostly organic produce in a renovated modern building. The people that live in this neighborhood recognize the importance of being able to enjoy a good conversation with their greengrocer and butcher.

marheinekeplatz/bergmannstrasse, www.meine-markthalle.de, t: 03061286146, open mon-fri 8am-8pm, sat 8am-6pm, u-bahn u7 gneisenaustrasse

㉘ Long **Bergmannstrasse** is the beating heart of this part of Kreuzberg. It's a myriad of small shops, restaurants, and coffee houses. Make sure not to skip the adjoining Friesenstrasse when you visit the neighborhood. This steep little side street is where you'll find a *Brezel Bar* (pretzel shop), flower shop Flores Y Amores, children's shop Mjot, and Koko Schultz (environmentally-friendly design).

friesenstrasse/bergmannstrasse, u-bahn u7 gneisenaustrasse

MORE TO EXPLORE

③ Organic vegetables and herbs are now grown in the **Prinzessinnengarten** on what used to be a total wasteland. The garden in the middle of Kreuzberg is very popular with neighborhood locals and visitors alike. It's a great place to walk around, have a drink, or pick up some veggies or plants.

prinzenstrasse 35-38 / prinzessinnenstrasse 15, prinzessinnengarten.net, t: 017624332297, open apr-oct daily from 10am, café from 11am, u-bahn u8 moritzplatz

④ **Planet Modulor** is a new creative multipurpose building in Kreuzberg. It was initiated by Modulor, a shop selling art supplies. In 2011 the business moved into this building on Moritzplatz together with a number of other creative small businesses. Looking for breakfast or coffee? Head to **Parker Bowles.**

prinzenstrasse 85, www.planetmodulor.de, t: 030690360, open hours vary, modulor: mon-fri 9am-8pm, sat 10am-6pm, u-bahn u8 moritzplatz

⑱ The **Landwehrkanal** is about seven miles long and runs through Kreuzberg, Neukölln, Tiergarten, and Charlottenburg. Stroll along the water and cross back over Admiralbrücke. This bridge is bustling with young people, especially in the summer. Numerous restaurants and bars can be found on the Paul Lincke and Planufer sides, which make for a great evening out.

paul-lincke-ufer / planufer, u-bahn u1, u8 kottbusser tor

㉓ **Berliner Unterwelten** offers underground tours at different locations in town. Tour F goes through the **Fichte-Bunker,** a 19th-century gas holder used during World War II as an air-raid shelter for women and children. After 1945 it was temporarily a shelter for prisoners, elderly people, and even the homeless. From 1963 onwards it was used for food storage. Tickets are available at the door.

fichtestrasse 6, www.berliner-unterwelten.de, t: 03049910518, open tours sat-sun noon-2pm (german), thu 4pm (german) & 6pm (english), entrance €11, u-bahn u7 südstern

㉜ **Park am Gleisdreieck** has a west and an east side. Each side is separated by the train tracks (the park was built on the former rail yards). The park was a request from the neighborhood and is a place to walk, sit in the sun, chill on the grass, and play. It's being developed further, but at every entrance there's a sign showing what you can find and where.

möckernstrasse/schöneberger strasse (main entrances), www.gruen-berlin.de/parks-gaerten/park-am-gleisdreieck/, u-bahn u1, u2 gleisdreieck

WALK 6

NEUKÖLLN

ABOUT THE WALK

If you take the detour to Rixdorf, this walk becomes rather long, but you have the opportunity to visit edgy areas like the Schillerkiez. This part of Berlin is changing rapidly. New shops and restaurants come and go, so chances are you'll discover something new yourself or find that one of the listings in this guide is no longer there. If this is your first visit to Berlin, don't start with this walk, as its main focus is eating, drinking, and shopping.

THE NEIGHBORHOODS

Even with high unemployment, problems with integration, and crime, Neukölln is one of the more popular areas in Berlin. The northern part in particular, **Kreuzkölln**, is transforming quickly. At times the vibe can be somewhat grim, but during the day it's usually quiet and relaxed in this part of town.

Our walk starts at former airport Tempelhof, built by the Nazis. It's one of the few remainders of the bombastic architecture of the Third Reich. The old air fields are now a city park called **Tempelhofer Freiheit.** It gained immense popularity very quickly. Berliners come here from far and wide to skate, grill, or chill. In 2014 the residents voted against building plans, so for now it will stay the way it is.

The **Schillerkiez,** the area between Tempelhof and Hermannstrasse, is a good example of the current gentrification problems. Rents continue rising because of the ever-growing number of rich foreigners moving in. It's becoming increasingly less affordable for the original residents. Don't be surprised if you see graffiti saying things like, *"Yuppies raus"* (Yuppies get out) or *"Touris raus"* (Tourists go away). But on the upside, the influx of people also means a steady stream of new restaurants, new initiatives, and small independent shops. In short, there's always something interesting to explore.

Hermannstrasse isn't the prettiest of streets, with ugly facades and cheap shops. But at the end are Rixdorf and Richardplatz, which provide a real small-town feel. You'll slowly progress via Richardstrasse through the more busy and touristy northern part of Neukölln: Kreuzkölln. It's situated on the border of Kreuzberg and is much loved because of its many restaurants, galleries, pop-up stores, exciting bars that are almost invisible during the day, and young designers.

SHORT ON TIME? HERE ARE THE HIGHLIGHTS
+ TEMPELHOFER FREIHEIT + NOWKOELLN FLOWMARKT
+ RICHARDPLATZ + TURKISH MARKET + KINDL

TIPS

// Good walk
for experienced
Berlin visitors
// This neighborhood comes
to life later on in the day
// Not ideal on bike,
but not impossible

NEUKÖLLN

1. Tempelhofer Freiheit / Mmaah
2. Tempelhof
3. Café Engels
4. Aviatrix Atelier
5. Caligari
6. Schiller Burger / Schiller Bar / Wilhelm Tell
7. Pequod Books
8. Veist
9. Lavanderia Vecchia
10. Schankwirtschaft Laidak
11. KINDL
12. Neuköllner Oper
13. Richardplatz / Rixdorf / Museum im Böhmischen Dorf
14. Rixbox
15. Klunkerkranich
16. Shio
17. Gastón
18. BCR/DBR
19. Wesen
20. Dots café
21. Two and Two
22. Reuterstraße
23. Photoautomat
24. Fräulein Frost
25. Café Valentin
26. Katie's Blue Cat
27. Chicha
28. Nowkoelln Flowmarkt
29. Café Jacques
30. Brammibal's Donuts
31. Turkish market
32. Brückenfahrt
33. Ankerklause

LEGEND

>> SIGHTS & ATTRACTIONS
>> FOOD & DRINK
>> SHOPPING
>> MORE TO EXPLORE

WALK 6 DESCRIPTION (approx. 4.6 miles)

Start at Tempelhofer Freiheit ❶ and if you're on a bike, make sure to cycle across the old airfield. You can tour the buildings of Tempelhof ❷, but make sure to sign up beforehand. Walk onto Herrfurthstrasse, which runs perpendicular to the field. Have breakfast at Engels ❸ and pop your head into a creative gallery ❹. Turn right at Herrfurthplatz, go over the Schillerpromenade, and take the first left. You'll find some good Italian food right around here ❺. Take a left on Weise-strasse ❻. Go right at Selchower Strasse for books ❼ or vintage clothing ❽. Leave the Schillerkiez, cross busy Hermannstrasse, and take a left. A bit off the route, in a Hinterhof (courtyard), is a good Italian restaurant ❾. Head onto Boddinstrasse, which is much quieter. You can grab a beer ❿ or, a bit farther on, enjoy modern art in an old brewery ⓫. Walk until you reach Karl-Marx-Strasse, where you can take a left (to ⓯) or a right to visit Rixdorf. If you decide to go right, walk down Karl-Marx-Strasse alongside the opera ⓬ to Richardplatz in Rixdorf, an older part of the city ⓭. Then follow Richardstrasse ⓮ and then Karl-Marx-Strasse. Walk straight on for a view of Klunkerkranich from a roof terrace ⓯. Turn right on Fuldastrasse. Take the first left, Donaustrasse, and then turn right onto Weichselstrasse. Now you've reached the more creative part of Neukölln, with many cafés and restaurants, and also some fashion shops ⓰. Walk until Weichselstrasse intersects with Weserstrasse. At the corner with the tapas bar ⓱ go left ⓲ ⓳ ⓴. Take another left at the intersection with Pannier-strasse for a small restaurant and cake ㉑. The walk continues straight from here. At the intersection with Reuterstrasse ㉒ you'll find many galleries. Go a bit farther on Weserstrasse and have your picture taken in the Photoautomat ㉓. Take a right on Friedelstrasse for some delicious ice cream ㉔, or turn left along the way for Swedish treats ㉕. Continue until you reach Maybachufer. You'll pass many food and drink options ㉖ ㉗. If you're lucky, the Nowkoelln Flowmarkt will be on ㉘. Take a left for the classic Café Jacques ㉙, walk along the water, and get a donut ㉚. A Turkish market is held here on Tuesdays and Fridays ㉛. Get on a canal boat ㉜ or have a drink at Ankerklause ㉝.

SIGHTS & ATTRACTIONS

② **Tempelhof** used to be Berlin's central airport. Building started in the 1920s, and in the 1930s, the Nazis expanded it to become the largest building in the world. During the Cold War, American airplanes landed here to bring food and goods to the cut off city. The *Luftbrücke* (airlift, 1948-1949) is commemorated with a monument in front of the building. In 2008, Tempelhof airport was closed and the space became a venue for fairs, festivals, and events. Tours of the building are offered.

platz der luftbrücke 5, www.tempelhoferfreiheit.de, t: 030200037441, see website for tour times, tour €13, u-bahn u6 platz der luftbrücke

⑪ **KINDL** is housed in the former Berlin Kindl-Bier brewery. The large building, with a brick tower and high windows, was built in the 1920s in German Expressionism style. After the brewery moved to a location outside of town, it became the *Zentrum für Zeitgenössische Kunst* (Center for Contemporary Art), with almost 66,000 square feet of exhibition space. This is a special place—check out the program on their website.

am sudhaus 2, www.kindl-berlin.de, t: 030832159120, see website, u-bahn u8 boddinstrasse, u7 rathaus neukölln

⑬ It wasn't until 1920 that Neukölln became part of Berlin. Before then it was an independent municipality, and until 1912 it was known as Rixdorf. The neighborhood is known for the Bohemian refugees it took in during the 18th century. The **Museum im Böhmischen Dorf** (open irregularly) is located in Kirchgasse alleyway just past **Richardplatz,** which is now the heart of **Rixdorf.** On this square are a few houses that suggest what Berlin used to look like. Walk around the neighborhood or have a drink on the green square. There's a *Weihnachtsmarkt* at Christmas.

richardplatz, www.museumimboehmischendorf.de, open museum thu 2pm-7pm, every 1st and 3rd Sunday of the month noon-2pm, u-bahn u7 karl-marx-strasse

FOOD & DRINK

③ **Café Engels** in the Schillerkiez is a great place for coffee, cake, a hearty breakfast, or lunch. Inside is whimsical and cozy, and if you want to engage in some people watching, the sidewalk café is the perfect spot.

herrfurthstrasse 21, facebook café-engels, t: 03064499067, open daily 9am-2am, price €4, u-bahn u8 boddinstrasse

⑤ Hole-in-the-wall Italian bar and bistro **Caligari** is understated and stylish, with its white walls and beautiful wooden furniture. The menu changes daily, with many vegetarian dishes, all for very reasonable prices. They are planning "culinary experiments" (supper clubs) with different guest chefs.

kienitzer strasse 110, www.caligariberlin.de, t: 03052649841, open daily 6pm-11pm, price €7, u-bahn u8 leinestrasse

⑥ What do you call a bar/annex *Backstube* (bakery)/burger joint in the Schillerkiez? Schiller, of course, named after a German writer. **Schiller Burger** bakes its own buns. Next door, with the entrance on the corner, is the **Schiller Bar,** where you can order a delicious breakfast or lunch. The attached restaurant **Wilhelm Tell** is more upscale, and the line between the two venues can be hard to determine. Make sure to check which menu you will be ordering from.

herrfurthstrasse 7 / weisestrasse 40, www.schillerbar.com, t: 01525808490, burger joint open daily noon-midnight, bar 9am-midnight, price burger €5, lunch €8, u-bahn u8 boddinstrasse

⑨ Italian restaurant **Lavanderia Vecchia** is located in an old laundromat, hidden away in the second *Hinterhof* (courtyard). The table linens on the ceiling are a reminder of the original purpose of the building—similar to the streets of Naples. They serve lunch, but their dinner is better. Dinner is a set menu that is posted online every week, known to be deliciously waist-expanding. You will always start with an assortment of antipasti.

flughafenstrasse 46, www.lavanderiavecchia.de, t: 03062722152, open tue-fri noon-2:30pm & 7:30pm-11pm, sat 7:30pm-11pm, price lunch €5-13, dinner menu incl. wine, water, and coffee €58, u-bahn u8 boddinstrasse, u7 rathaus neukölln

(10) A *Schankwirtschaft* is a café that serves alcohol and nothing else. But **Schankwirtschaft Laidak** is different: They also serve breakfast. It's an old-fashioned, homey place with leather couches, bookshelves, and wobbly lamp shades. This part of Neukölln is relatively quiet. The little square across from Laidak is pretty, and so are the facades of the houses around it.
boddinstrasse 42, www.laidak.net, open mon-sat from noon, sun from 10am, price €2.50, u-bahn u8 boddinstrasse, u7 rathaus neukölln

(14) There is no simpler way to fill an empty square than with a large, boxlike construction with a bar inside and unfinished wooden benches and tables underneath green umbrellas. **Rixbox** sells cakes, sandwiches, street food, and other sweet treats. This venue is a pleasant surprise between quiet Richardstrasse and ugly Karl-Marx-Strasse.
richardstrasse 2, www.rixbox.de, open mon-sat 8am-9pm, sun noon-6pm, price €4, u-bahn u7 rathaus neukölln

(17) **Gastón** serves great tapas and great wine in an upbeat atmosphere. It's busy, noisy, and alive. You'll sit at tiny tables and, even if you've made reservations for your party of four, you may still end up sitting in a row at the bar. Sundays are for paella and sangria—be prepared for an authentic experience.
weichselstrasse 18, www.gaston-tapasbar.com, t: 01628199853, open daily 3pm-2am, price tapas €4, u-bahn u7, u8 hermannplatz

(20) Fresh and organic is the name of the game at **Dots café.** They serve hearty breakfast all day. From pancakes, scrambled eggs, and hash browns to a classic German *Frühstücksteller* (breakfast). They make everything from scratch and their homemade *gravad lachs* (cured salmon) comes highly recommended.
weserstrasse 191, www.ilovedots.de, t: 03062725131, open mon-fri 11am-6pm, sat-sun 9am-7pm (kitchen closes at 4pm), price €5, u-bahn u8 hermannplatz

(21) **Two and Two** is a cozy place that sells French sweets and Japanese stationery, paper, and pens. Owners Eri and Tose are from Paris and Tokyo. Select your coffee or tea from a handwritten menu.
pannierstrasse 6, www.twoandtwoberlin.com, t: 03053791578, open daily 10am-6:30pm, price €4, u-bahn u7, u8 hermannplatz

㉔ On average, Germans eat 110 scoops of ice cream per person, per year. That's two scoops per week. Want to join the fun? Creamery **Fräulein Frost** is a great place to start. It's large, busy, and bustling. All their ice cream is organic and they have a huge selection of unique flavors.

friedelstrasse 39, t: 03095595521, open mon-fri from 1pm, sat-sun from noon, u-bahn u8 schönleinstrasse

㉕ At the tiny Swedish **Café Valentin** you can order all kinds of porridge and *smorrebrot* (open-face sandwiches). It feels like you're walking into someone's living room, and the smell of cinnamon buns is irresistible—try one.

sanderstrasse 13, www.cafevalentin.de, open wed-sat 10am-4pm, sun 11am-6pm, price €4, u-bahn u8 schönleinstrasse

㉖ When Canadian Olivia Wood and Vietnamese Ngoc Duong opened **Katie's Blue Cat** in 2011, it was an immediate favorite with locals in the neighborhood. The homemade sweets are tempting and the Bonanza coffee is excellent. The assortment is both American and English and varies from cheesecake and vegan pastries to gluten-free cookies and scones.

friedelstrasse 31, www.katiesbluecat.de, t: 01788069701, open mon-fri 8:30am-6:30pm, sat-sun 10am-7pm, price cake €3, u-bahn u8 schönleinstrasse

㉗ At **Chicha,** it's all about Peruvian food and *pisco* (Peruvian firewater). The specialty is the *ceviche*—pieces of fish cooked in citrus juices—but there are a number of other delicious dishes on the menu. There are no starters or main courses—just order an assortment of small dishes. Top it off with a nice cocktail—their *Pisco Sour* is the best in town.

friedelstrasse 34, www.chicha-berlin.de, t: 03062731010, open wed-sun 6pm-midnight, price €9, u-bahn u8 schönleinstrasse

㉙ **Café Jacques** opened its doors almost 20 years ago. It moved around the corner in 2014, but didn't lose its faithful regulars. They serve dishes like saddle of veal with pistachio nuts and cognac sauce, and red beets with goat cheese. Couscous is on the menu twice a week, and the wine list is phenomenal.

maybachufer 14, t: 0306941048, open daily from 6pm, price €15, u-bahn u8 schönleinstrasse

③⓪ **Brammibal's Donuts** started in Markthalle Neun, but because their donuts were so popular they decided to open their own store. Choose from over 20 flavors, including pear, pumpkin, pretzels with chocolate, and raspberry with almonds. All the donuts are vegan. They also serve bagels with vegan toppings. Try one of their homemade lemonades; the lavender-lime flavor is delicious.
maybachufer 8, www.brammibalsdonuts.com, t: 03023948455, open tue-sun 10am-7pm, price €3, u-bahn u8 schönleinstrasse

③③ It's always busy in the iconic **Ankerklause.** Once a rundown bar reminiscent of a rough sailors' dive, it quickly became one of the best party places in the neighborhood after being discovered by a younger and more artistic crowd. Thursday nights are for dancing, and on the weekend they serve breakfast until 4pm while playing reggae, indie rock, or hip-hop.
kottbusser damm 104, www.ankerklause.de, t: 0306935649, open mon 4pm-4am, tue-sun 10am-4am, price €5, u-bahn u8 schönleinstrasse

SHOPPING

④ Art, clothing, and coffee—**Aviatrix Atelier** has it all. What sets this studio apart is their philosophy that kids and artists can inspire each other. They occasionally have artists-in-residence whose works, as well as those of the founders, are for sale.
herrfurthstrasse 13, www.aviatrixatelier.com, t: 03052663089, open daily noon-8pm, u-bahn u8 boddinstrasse

⑦ In an area with many international residents, an international secondhand bookstore comes as no surprise. **Pequod Books** sells titles in as many as 15 different languages. Browse through the large selection as long as you like—the owners want you to find the book that's right for you.
selchower strasse 33, facebook pequodbooks, t: 015255130374, open mon-sat 1pm-7pm, u-bahn u8 boddinstrasse

⑧ **Veist** is one of the prettiest shops in this neighborhood. They sell consignment items with a story and also offer rentable items. If you're attending a party

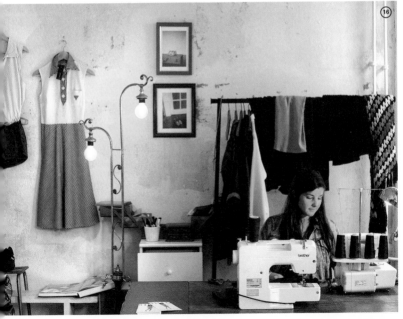

(16)

in Berlin but don't want to buy a dress, rent one from Veist (arrange beforehand via the website).

selchower strasse 32, www.veistberlin.com, t: 03095606251, open wed-sat 2pm-7pm, u-bahn u8 boddinstrasse

⑯ **Shio** is a tiny place in Kreuzkölln, the hippest part of Neukölln. It's a good place for upcycling (creative reuse of recycled clothing), handmade fashion, and vintage. They also sell fashion from up-and-coming Berlin designers, jewelry, and accessories. If you want to bring home something special, this is where you'll find it.

weichselstrasse 59, www.shiostore.com, open mon-sat 1pm-7pm, u-bahn u7, u8 hermannplatz, u7 rathaus neukölln

⑱ This combination record shop and clothing store is well established in a country that loves acronyms. **DBR** stands for Down By Retro and offers vintage clothing, unique skincare products, and stunning jewelry. **BCR** stands for Bass Cadet Records, and their shelves are filled with vinyl—it's heaven for old-school music lovers.

weserstrasse 189, www.downbyretro.com, www.basscadetrecords.com, open mon 2pm-8pm, tue-thu 11am-8pm, fri 11am-9pm, sat 2pm-9pm, u-bahn u7, u8 hermannplatz

⑲ At **Wesen** you'll find organic and environmentally-friendly clothing from local designers. You'll find no felt A-line skirts, but rather beautiful clothes as a counter-movement to the disposable fashion we see nowadays. Everything is made in Berlin and Brandenburg.

weserstrasse 191, www.wesen-berlin.com, t: 03054592277, open mon-sat 11am-7pm, u-bahn u7, u8 hermannplatz

MORE TO EXPLORE

① Tempelhof airport closed its doors forever in 2008. A year later, the old airport opened to visitors as **Tempelhofer Freiheit** park. Where once Raisin Bombers used to land during the airlift of 1948 and 1949, you can now take a stroll, bike, skate, or Segway ride. You can also picnic on the 740-acre terrain. At Columbia-damm you'll find **Mmaah,** which sells grilled Korean dishes.

main entrances on the tempelhofer damm, columbiadamm and oderstrasse, www.tempelhoferfreiheit.de, open daily dawn till dusk, free entrance, s-bahn tempelhof, u-bahn u6 platz der luftbrücke, u8 boddinstrasse

⑫ The **Neuköllner Oper** is a progressive, creative, and modern opera house. This is not the place to see a classic opera. Entrances are on Karl-Marx-Strasse and Richardstrasse. The building itself is very beautiful and worth a look, even if you don't plan to see a performance.

karl-marx-strasse 131-133, www.neukoellneroper.de, t: 03068890777, see website for program and prices, u-bahn u7 karl-marx-strasse

⑮ Roof terraces are perfect for bars. While most only open at night, **Klunker-kranich** is open all day. Getting there does take some effort: Enter Neukölln Arcaden mall through the Postbank/library entrance, take the elevator to the fifth floor, and walk up the stairs to the sixth floor. Once on top, you'll have a magnificent view of Berlin. It's like a city beach, but up in the air. The terrace is closed in January and February.

karl-marx-strasse 66, www.klunkerkranich.de, open may-sep mon-sat starting 10am, sun starting noon, mar-apr & oct-dec thu-fri starting 4pm, sat-sun starting noon, u-bahn u7 rathaus neukölln

㉒ Neukölln is filled with small galleries with irregular hours. *Vernissages* (art exhibition opening events) are announced online. Several galleries are located on **Reuterstrasse** and around Reuterplatz. Have a good look around this street because new and interesting places open up all the time. A few names to re-member are ReTramp, Galerie R31, and Holz Kohlen Koks.

reuterstrasse, u-bahn u7, u8 hermannplatz

㉓ Dig a €2 coin out of your pocket for one of best souvenirs in Berlin: a series of four different passport pictures in the **Photoautomat.** These machines are dotted throughout the city, such as at the Prater Biergaten (Prenzlauer Berg) and the Warschauer Brücke (Friedrichshain).

weserstrasse 7, www.photoautomat.de, price €2, u-bahn u7, u8 hermannplatz

㉘ The **Nowkoelln Flowmarkt,** located along the Landwehrkanal on the May-bachufer, is different from most flea markets. Browse around for some unique vintage or homemade finds, have a taco or other snack, and listen to live music alongside the water. It's a great place for a relaxing afternoon.

maybachufer, between friedelstrasse and nansenstrasse, www.nowkoelln.de, open every other week sun 10am-6pm (closed in winter), u-bahn u8 schönleinstrasse

㉛ The **Turkish market** on the Maybachufer makes you feel like you've been transported to a real Turkish bazaar. Women in long colorful dresses walk around with pounds of fruits and vegetables, and every stall has something different to offer, including mangos, medlar (a flowering fruit), herbs, bread, and *börek* (phyllo-dough pastry). Just before the stalls close, remaining goods are sold for bargain prices.

maybachufer, www.tuerkenmarkt.de, open tue & fri 11am-6:30pm, u-bahn u8 schönleinstrasse

㉜ Tired of walking? Hop aboard a Reederi Riedel boat tour. The **Brückenfahrt** is different from most boat tours in Berlin. Yes, it's long (14 miles and about 3.5 hours), but you really see all the sights and you pass 64 bridges!

kottbusser brücke (next to ankerklause), www.reederei-riedel.de, t: 03067961470, price €21, u-bahn u8 schönleinstrasse

WITH MORE TIME

The walks in this book will take you to most of the city's main highlights. Of course, there are still a number of places worth visiting that are not included in these walks. We have listed a few of these below. Note that not all of these places are easily accessible by foot from town, but you can reach them all using public transportation.

Ⓐ The **Olympiastadion** was built to host the 1936 Olympic Games during the Nazi reign. Because of this, the building, designed by architect Werner March, has a typical bombastic Nazi look.

olympischer platz 3, westend, www.olympiastadion-berlin.de, open daily from 9am (nov-mar from 10am), close depending on the season, entrance €7, tour €11, s-bahn, u-bahn u2 olympiastadion

Ⓑ A derelict tower is the main attraction of the **Teufelsberg.** This "mountain" is situated in **Grunewald,** a large forest just west of Berlin. The hill was built by the Allies, who transported all the debris from World War II to this area outside the city. The towers were erected by the NSA—the US National Security Agency—and were the largest listening stations in the British zone. There is a lot of history here and it is a beautiful place to walk. Check the website for tours.

teufelsseechaussee 10, www.berliner-teufelsberg.com, price tour starting at €7, s-bahn messe süd of heerstrasse

Ⓒ If you want to escape the rush of the city, a walk around the **Schlachtensee** does the trick. Everyone in need of some fresh air walks around this large lake, from people with dogs to runners. On the east side is **Die Fischerhütte am Schlachtensee,** which has a large patio where you can eat and drink. From here you can take Schillerstrasse to the **Haus am Waldsee.** This museum is beautifully located in a park on a pond. They usually have interesting exhibitions and you can have a drink and a bite in the idyllic garden. Take the U-Bahn back into the city.

museum: argentinische allee 30, www.hausamwaldsee.de, t: 0308018935, open hours vary, entrance €7, s-bahn schlachtensee, u-bahn u3 krumme lanke

(D) Dahlem is an upscale neighborhood of Berlin. This is where you'll find the **Botanischer Garten** (Botanical Garden), **Botanisches Museum** (Botanical Museum), and the **Königliche Gartenakademie** (Royal Garden Academy). The garden and museum belong together and will help you learn all about the world of plants. The Königliche Gartenakademie used to educate royal gardeners. Now they sell stunning plants and garden accessories in one of the greenhouses.
königin-luise-strasse 6-8 / altensteinstrasse 15a, dahlem, www.bgbm.org, www.koenigliche-gartenakademie.de, t: 03083850100, garden open daily from 9am, museum 10am-6pm, price garden €6, museum €2.50, s-bahn botanischer garten, u-bahn u3 dahlem-dorf, u9 rathaus steglitz

(E) **Wedding** is a rapidly up-and-coming neighborhood in Mitte, along the river Panke. It is home to a vibrant artists' community with many galleries. Right now it's still a bit too fragmented to create a full walk for the purposes of this guide, but you can go and explore along the river Panke.
s-bahn, u-bahn u6 wedding

Ⓕ Until the end of the 19th century the **Hamburger Bahnhof** was the main stop for trains between Berlin and Hamburg. Soon after it closed, it became a museum of modern art: **Museum für Gegenwart.**

invalidenstrasse 50-51, www.smb.museuml, t: 030266424242, open tue-wed & fri 10am-6pm, thu 10am-8pm, sat-sun 11am-6pm, entrance €10, u-bahn u6 naturkundemuseum, s-bahn hauptbahnhof

Ⓖ **Tiergarten** is the largest park in Berlin. It's great for a walk, but you can also rent a rowboat and take to the waters of Neuer See lake, close to the large *Biergarten*. In the middle of Tiergarten is the **Siegessäule,** a golden goddess who appears in the German movie *Der Himmel über Berlin (Wings of Desire)*. Climb the 285 steps of the column and enjoy the view.

grosser stern, strasse des 17. juni, tiergarten, t: 0303912961, open siegessäule apr-oct mo-fri 9:30am-6:30pm, sat-sun 9:30am-7pm, nov-mar mon-fri 10am-5pm, sat-sun 10am-5:30pm, entrance €3, s-bahn bellevue

Ⓗ In the area around Potsdamer Platz is the **Kulturforum,** built in the 1950s and 1960s. The **Philharmonie,** next door, is one of the most renowned concert halls in the world. On Tuesdays at 1pm they have a free lunch concert (not in summer). The Kulturforum also houses the **Neue Nationalgalerie** for modern art in a building designed by Mies van der Rohe, and the **Neue Staatsbibliothek** (Berlin State Library).

matthäikirchplatz, tiergarten, www.kulturforum-berlin.com, see website for times and prices, s-bahn, u-bahn u2 potsdamer platz

Ⓘ **Viktoriapark,** with its artificial waterfalls, was created between 1884 and 1894. It's located on the hill in the Kreuzberg neighborhood. On the top of the hill is a large cross—a neo-gothic monument commemorating the Prussian victory over Napoleon. From here you have an amazing view of the city. Have a picnic in the park or enjoy a beer in **Golgatha Biergarten.**

kreuzbergstrasse, open daily, u-bahn u6 platz der luftbrücke

Ⓙ **Volkspark Friedrichshain** was the first park in Berlin for the commoners in the 19th century. The *Märchenbrunnen* (fairytale fountains) from 1913 are the highlight: They're a Neo-Baroque complex of springs and gardens with statues inspired by the fairytales of the Brothers Grimm. Many Berliners come here to cool down on a hot day. The park itself is used to barbecue, run, relax, or catch a movie in the open-air cinema.

am friedrichshain, open daily, u-bahn u2 senefelderplatz, u5 strausberger platz

(K) The former Standort Haus 1, once the workplace of Stasi minister Erich Mielke, is now the oppressive **Stasimuseum.** Beginning in 1990 the building was occupied by demonstrators and shortly after, the old offices were sealed off. Time literally stood still here: The furniture is straight from the GDR era. They have permanent and temporary exhibitions about the practices of the Stasi.

ruschestrasse 103, haus 1, lichtenberg, www.stasimuseum.de, t: 0305536854, mon-fri 10am-6pm, sat-sun 11am-6pm, entrance €6, u-bahn u5 magdalenenstrasse, s-bahn frankfurter allee

(L) **Schlesischer Busch** is a great part of town full of bars and restaurants. In 2014 the famous **White Trash club** moved here. To the southeast is **Treptower Park,** a large, green area on the banks of the river Spree. And don't miss **Sowjetisches Ehrenmal Treptow.** This enormous statue is one of the three monuments commemorating the more than 80,000 fallen Russian soldiers after Berlin was liberated in 1945. North of the park is **Insel der Jugend,** with a cultural center and a café.

schlesischer busch / puschkinallee, s-bahn treptower park

AFTER DARK

When it comes to nightlife, Berlin has something for everyone. Clubs come alive around midnight, and don't be surprised to see long lines at legendary clubs like Tresor or Berghain as late (or early) as 3am.

Not much of a party animal? There are many other things you can do, such as catch a movie in GDR monument Kino International or one of the living-room cinemas. Afterwards have a locally brewed beer in a bar like Hops & Barley or Kaschk. Or, opt for a delicious cocktail.

In the mood for a more cultural adventure? In addition to the larger venues, there are many smaller places that guarantee a great night out, such as Piano Salon Christophori, which has piano concerts. You can find the latest information about nightlife in Berlin on **www.timetomomo.com,** from swanky cocktail bars and popular wine bars to local pubs and popular clubs.

HOTELS

A good bed, a tasty breakfast, and a nice interior: These are all the ingredients for a pleasant hotel stay. Even more important, however, might be location. A hotel is really only good if you can walk out of the lobby and straight into the bustling city.

Berlin is a diverse city. Want to see all the major sights? Get a hotel in Charlottenburg or Mitte. From the 25hours Hotel you'll have a magnificent view of the Tiergarten. Or would you rather go shopping and have some drinks at one of the many sidewalk cafés? A hotel in Prenzlauer Berg or the Scheunenviertel in Mitte is your best bet. Hotel Amano is in the middle of the Berlin fashion district. If you've come to Berlin to party, Kreuzberg and Friedrichshain are the neighborhoods for you. The hip Michelberger Hotel will be right up your alley. Go to **www.timetomomo.com** for more information about hotels in Berlin.

WWW.TIMETOMOMO.COM

OUR PERSONAL SELECTION OF HOTELS IN THE HOTTEST NEIGHBORHOODS IN TOWN. GO ONLINE & CLICK TO BOOK.

INDEX

MOON BERLIN WALKS

FIRST EDITION

Avalon Travel
An imprint of Perseus Books
A Hachette Book Group company
1700 Fourth Street
Berkeley, CA 94710, USA
www.moon.com

ISBN 978-1-63121-596-4

Concept & Original Publication "time to momo Berlijn" © 2017 by mo'media.
All rights reserved.
For the latest on time to momo walks and recommendations, visit www.timetomomo.com.

MO'MEDIA

TEXT & WALKS
Maartje van Ours

TRANSLATION
Cindi Sheridan-Heller

MAPS
Van Oort redactie & kartografie

PHOTOGRAPHY
Petra de Hamer, Marjolein den Hartog

DESIGN
Studio 100% & Oranje Vormgevers

PROJECT EDITORS
Heleen Ferdinandusse
Bambi Bogert

AVALON TRAVEL

PROJECT EDITOR
Sierra Machado

COPY EDITOR
Maggie Ryan

PROOFREADER
Megan Mulholland

COVER DESIGN
Derek Thornton, Faceout Studios

Printed in China by RR Donnelley
First U.S. printing, September 2017.

100%
good
time

time to momo

BERLIN

And to find out more about
the latest hot spots, best
hotels, nicest neighborhoods,
and where to have the most
fun in Berlin, go to
www.timetomomo.com/berlin

Individual
walks

app

time to momo
MAP APP

Download your free time to momo app from
www.timetomomo.com/apps, and know your way
around town. For more information, go to:

www.timetomomo.com/mapapp

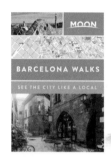

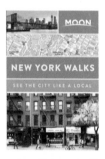
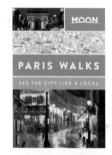
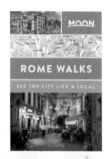